THE
SEARCH
FOR
CHRISTIAN
CREDIBILITY

THE
SEARCH
FOR
CHRISTIAN
CREDIBILITY
Explorations in Contemporary Belief

ALVIN C. PORTEOUS

ABINGDON PRESS

nashville and new york

THE SEARCH FOR CHRISTIAN CREDIBILITY

Copyright © 1971 by Abingdon Press

ISBN 0-687-37121-X
Library of Congress Catalog Card Number: 74-148069

Scripture quotations unless otherwise noted are from
the Revised Standard Version of the Bible, copy-
righted 1946 and 1952 by the Division of Christian
Education, National Council of Churches, and are
used by permission.

Scripture quotations noted NEB are from the New
English Bible, New Testament. © the Delegates of
the Oxford University Press and the Syndics of the
Cambridge University Press 1961. Reprinted by permission.

Selections from James H. Cone, *Black Theology
and Black Power,* copyright © 1969 by The Seabury
Press.

SET UP, PRINTED, AND BOUND BY THE
PARTHENON PRESS, AT NASHVILLE,
TENNESSEE, UNITED STATES OF AMERICA

for
PAUL
SHARON
and
CAROL
whose generation demands a credible faith

PREFACE

The theology of the last decade has been marked by an unprecedented variety of experimentations and innovations which have involved, in many cases, a radical recasting of basic Christian belief. New theological thrusts have appeared in bewildering profusion—"honest-to-God" theology, secular theology, "death-of-God" theology, hermeneutical theology, theology of hope—all concerned with the monumental task of rehabilitating the credibility of the Christian message in a cultural milieu increasingly unreceptive to its truth-claims. Depending on one's point of view, this sudden proliferation of theological options represents either a debilitating identity crisis which presages the final demise of theology, or a remarkable surge of theological creativity which promises to breathe new life into the moribund structures of Christian belief.

I am inclined to opt for the latter assessment. This book is offered as a modest addition to the continuing search for Christian credibility to which so many fertile minds contributed during the sixties. It reflects an attempt to enter into dialogue with some of the most promising of the recent theological movements as well as the giants of the last generation whose thought I examined in my earlier book, *Prophetic Voices in Contemporary Theology*. The discerning reader will note a particular indebtedness to the theology of hope and the theology of the secular, as well as the thought of Dietrich Bonhoeffer, Paul Tillich, and Reinhold Niebuhr.

Any theology which is to satisfy the canons of contemporary credibility must take adequate notice of its social and cultural *sitz im leben* which defines for it the context for responsible theologizing. I have sought in these theological explorations to do full justice to the following contextual factors: the radical secularization of our age;

the urgent quest of many in our day for a new style of humanness; the ubiquity of revolution in our world, spearheaded by the black, the young, and the poor; the pervasive orientation to the future in our culture; the decadence of traditional religious language and symbols which have lost their communicative power; and finally, but not least importantly, the church's massive betrayal of its Christian mission in our time.

Many friends, students, and colleagues have contributed the stimulation and insight which has made this book possible. In particular, I would like to record my warm appreciation to the following: Professor Jürgen Moltmann, whose influence on my thinking is much in evidence on these pages, and whose friendly hospitality did so much to make my 1967–68 sabbatical year at the University of Tübingen delightful and rewarding; Professor Warren L. Molton, colleague on the Central Baptist Theological Seminary faculty, whose probing questions, insightful criticisms, and sustaining friendship made this a better book than it would otherwise have been; and my wife, Marion, who shared in the struggle and search which is reflected in these pages, and without whose faith, hope, and love, this work would not have come to fruition.

Alvin C. Porteous
Kansas City, Kansas

August 24, 1970

CONTENTS

PART ONE

INTRODUCTION

I

THE CREDIBILITY GAP
IN CONTEMPORARY BELIEF

We need no one to remind us that ours is not one of the great ages of faith. It may, in fact, be the case that our particular generation has witnessed a de-escalation of faith which has few if any precedents in all the centuries of Christian history. The robust and revolutionary beliefs of a bygone age—the ringing affirmations concerning a living God creatively and redemptively at work in his world—the militant convictions which fueled the revolutionary movement of the early Christians and sent them out to "turn the world upside down"—these do not come easily and convincingly to the lips of contemporary Christians. They have been largely scaled down in our day to harmless assertions of pious trivia. Assimilated and co-opted by the conventional wisdom of our materialistic culture, they have lost their bite and their scandal. They continue to provide, to be sure, what Marx once referrred to as "a hot-water bottle for some individual souls." But for increasing numbers of twentieth-century men and women they elicit only a polite, if somewhat amused, tolerance. They inspire, at best, the kind of mild curiosity and nostalgic reminiscence which characterizes Sunday visitors to a museum.

The Crisis of Contemporary Belief

It would be a serious mistake to underestimate the radical and unparalleled nature of the crisis of Christian belief which has been burgeoning particularly during the last decade. For one thing, it has struck at the very jugular

15

vein of the Christian world view—its belief in God. When the credibility of any transcendent reality which can be appropriately called God is brought into question, as it is by many today, then the entire edifice of Christian belief is shaken to its foundations. For when the reality of God is subject to radical doubt, all other articles of Christian belief are rendered vulnerable, and the entire enterprise of theology begins to look suspect.

Equally unsettling is the fact that this radical questioning of the most fundamental of religious beliefs is occurring today in the bosom of the church's own fellowship. For centuries the church has had to mount an apologetic to deal with the skepticism of an unbelieving secular world. What is new today is that the radical skeptic is found no longer among those whom Schleiermacher called "the cultured despisers of religion." He is found in the ranks of the friends of religion, among a growing number of laymen, clergy, and theologians of the church who are fighting a desperate battle to make their Christian faith credible to themselves as well as to others. The newness of this situation has been well described by Langdon Gilkey in a recent book: "The Church itself, the religious community itself, through the experience and reflective thought of its official representatives and functionaries, is not so much expounding 'faith' to a doubting world as it is itself exploring the depths of its own uncertainty, and itself searching for possible foundations for its language, its worship, and its works. This *is* new, and it is radical." [1]

The explorations of Christian belief contained in this book attempt to face realistically this internal crisis of theological meaning in the church which threatens to undermine the credibility of its witness. They are not offered as the *ex cathedra* judgments of a writer who is himself

[1] *Naming the Whirlwind: The Renewal of God-Language* (Indianapolis: Bobbs-Merrill, 1969), pp. 9-10.

untouched by the fires of modern doubt and secularity. They represent, rather, the embattled confessional statements of one who is fighting for his own theological life. They are an attempt to salvage from the Christian theological heritage those things which can honestly be believed by a truly modern man in a radically secular age.

For some, what follows may seem like rather lean fare, indeed. As a matter of fact, it is meant to be "bread and butter theology." There is little here for those who like to indulge in the luxury of high-flying metaphysical speculation or exhaustively comprehensive systematization. This is theology "for the road," subsistence theology, if you will, designed to sustain the modern Christian on his worldly journey where clearly marked signposts are hard to find and dead-end roads are difficult to avoid. It is "pilgrim theology" forged out of the crucible of a continuing dialogue between biblical faith and the rapidly unfolding events of our revolutionary time.

Ronald Knox once taunted William Temple for paying too much attention to modern skepticism, all the time asking "What will Jones swallow?" Temple's rejoinder, I believe, expresses the mood of many contemporary Christians: "I am Jones, asking what there is to eat." To ask for something that is *edible,* when it comes to Christian belief, is to ask for something that is at least *credible.* "We are twentieth-century men," Gordon Kaufman reminds us, "who know modern physics and psychoanalysis, communist tyranny and Hiroshima, Freud and Marx, Einstein and Hitler; and we must seek to grasp God's historical act in Jesus Christ in terms *we* can understand and accept and believe." [2] Only a faith which commends itself to us as inherently credible can nourish us with the bread

---

[2] *Systematic Theology: A Historicist Perspective* (New York: Charles Scribner's Sons, 1968), p. 72.

of meaning and stimulate us with the wine of hope in an age threatened by both meaninglessness and hopelessness.

The Shock of Radical Change

On every side today we are reminded that the great new fact of our time is the outbreak of massive, cataclysmic, revolutionary change. Old worlds are breaking up before our very eyes and a radically new world—a world which some have called the postmodern world is convulsively coming to birth. Reigning cultures are being vigorously challenged by new experimental countercultures. It is not to be wondered at that in such a situation the credibility of traditional theological structures has been subjected to intolerable strains.

The traumatic birth pangs of a new age have taken most of us off guard and left us in a state of disorder and confusion, groping for familiar signposts which are no longer there. "History as it comes into our lives," writes Robert Heilbroner, a Harvard economics professor, "is charged with surprise and shock."

When we think back over the past few years what strikes us is the suddenness of its blows, the unannounced descent of its thunderbolts. Wars, revolutions, uprisings have burst upon us with terrible rapidity. Advances in science and technology have rewritten the very terms and conditions of the human contract, with no more warning than the morning headlines. Encompassing social and economic changes have not only unalterably rearranged our lives, but seem to have done so behind our backs, while we were not looking.[3]

What of the reaction of the church to these successive shock waves of radical change? The temptation to see itself

[3] *The Future as History* (New York: Harper & Brothers, 1960), p. 13.

as an island of stability in a sea of change is always a strong one. In a time of revolutionary upheaval such as ours, church people find it easy to reach out wistfully for the assurances of timeless and changeless structures of belief. The "faith once and for all delivered to the saints" has an irresistible appeal. The church becomes a sanctuary to which people flee from the apocalyptic fire-storms of modern life. The Gospel becomes an anodyne to soothe nerve ends jangled by incessant change and conflict. Theology becomes the protector of those eternal verities which alone are immune to the buffeting of historical change.

Those who embrace this image of the Christian faith as a bastion of changelessness in a changing world find emotional reinforcement for their beliefs in some of the popular hymnody of the church:

> In heavenly love abiding,
> No change my heart shall fear;
> And safe is such confiding,
> For nothing changes here.

Or,

> Change and decay in all around I see;
> O thou who changest not, abide with me.

Long sentimental attachment to such words make it difficult for us to see, on the one hand, how close they take us to the borders of heresy, and on the other, how expressive they are of a reactionary, defensive posture in the face of the crisis of modern belief. According to church historian Martin E. Marty, that crisis has been infecting the consciousness of Christians most decisively since the mid-nineteenth century. It has taken, he declares, the form of a threefold movement toward secularization—a frontal attack on gods and churches on the Continent ("utter secularity"); what might be called a "benign neglect" of Christian claims and teachings in England ("mere secularity"); and a subtly disguised transformation of Christian symbols, along with the retention of the external forms of religion, in the United States ("controlled secularity").[4]

This "modern schism," as Marty calls it, has caused poignant reverberations in the Christian consciousness. A typical expression of the psychological and spiritual trauma occasioned by it comes from the pen of a nineteenth century divine, Frederick Robertson: "It is an awful moment when the soul begins to find the props on which it has blindly rested so long are, many of them, rotten, and begins to suspect them all."[5] That reflects rather well the painful self-revelation which many still experience today as the abyss of unbelief opens up before them.

Many people react to this crisis of disintegrating credibility with an attempt to keep their fundamental belief-structures intact by a desperate effort of the will. They resort to what Tillich called the strategy of "reactive" literalism "which is aware of the questions but represses them, half consciously, half unconsciously."[6] Such forced attempts to allay their doubts about basic matters of belief are often buttressed by an uncritical appeal to the authority of church or Bible.

Authoritarian methods of holding the crisis of belief at bay are inevitably both destructive and futile. For one thing, they are profoundly damaging to a person's psychological and spiritual integrity. The stifling of honest questionings splits the personality at its center and purchases a fragile security at the price of surrendering genuine autonomy and maturity. Moreover, such methods

---

[4] *The Modern Schism* (London: SCM Press, 1969).
[5] Quoted in *ibid.*, p. 94.
[6] Paul Tillich, *Dynamics of Faith* (New York: Harper & Brothers, 1957), p. 53.

are never really successful in shoring up the rotting tim-
bers of the house of faith. Once the termites of doubt have
begun to eat away at the foundations, no arbitrary appeal
to authority can rehabilitate the structures of belief in their
original form. Authoritarian suppression of doubt may
for a time restore a measure of subjective credibility to
one's beliefs. But the security gained thereby is more apparent than real. Only increasingly fanatical and willful
self-deception can stave off the final collapse of faith.

Continuity and Change in Christian Belief

The search for Christian credibility requires a stance of
openness and flexibility with respect to the symbols and
belief-structures which define for us the meaning of our
Christian faith. A faith-perspective that is not vulnerable
to change can scarcely be expected to survive the rigors
of today's revolutionary world. This does not mean that
the demands of credibility necessitate a wholesale jettison-
ing of tradition. On the contrary, the achievement of Christian credibility always entails a delicate balance between
past traditions and contemporary relevance, a dynamic
combination of both continuity and change. A question
posed by Norbert Wiener (the man who invented the word
"cybernetics") admirably lays out for us the parameters
of our theological task today: "How can man change what
he has loved the most—including his religion—without
destroying what is still to be loved in it?" [7]

In order to do justice to the elements of both continuity
and change in the formulating of Christian belief, our
theological reflections must keep in fruitful tension all
three modes of time—past, present, and future. Faithful-

[7] Quoted by Donald W. Shriver, "Continuity and Change in Society and
Theology" in *Theology Today*, January, 1969, p. 420.

ness of these time dimensions dictates a threefold norm for all theological work.

There is, first of all, the *historical* norm. This requires that our contemporary theological formulations maintain a meaningful continuity with the sources of Christian faith in the Bible and Christian tradition. According to this norm, a particular statement of belief can be adjudged "Christian" only when it reflects the basic intentionality, if not the precise terminology, of the original community of believers who witnessed to God's revelatory action in Jesus Christ. Fidelity to this norm is our only safeguard against the peril of purchasing a cheap kind of credibility which sacrifices an authentically Christian substance.

Next, there is the *existential* or *experiential* norm of theology. This calls upon us to show how the originative reports and symbols of the Christian faith illuminate the whole gamut of human experience in our present world. The Christ-event must be symbolized and represented in such a way as to "make sense" of the varied facets of modern man's existence, ranging from his personal and social problems to the many expressions of his intellectual and cultural life. A theology which fails to apply this norm with sufficient rigor loses its existential and experiential grounding and becomes abstract and irrelevant. Lacking specific referents to living, concrete experience, it strikes men of the twentieth century as incredible, however grandiose its claims of preserving the purity of first-century Christianity.

There is a third norm which has been much neglected in the history of Christian thought which is being re-emphasized in the current theologies of hope. We will refer to it as the *futurological* norm. This requires of us that we formulate our fundamental theological concepts in such a way that they "become not judgments which nail reality down to what it is, but anticipations which show reality in its prospects and its future possibilities." [8] Statements of belief must be, at one and the same time, expressions of hope. Theology must set forth a logic of Christian hope, specifying the ground and goal of our expectations for the future on the basis of which the insufficiency of past and present are judged. Christians are enjoined in Scripture: "Be ready always to give an answer to every man that asketh you a reason of the hope that is in you." (I Pet. 3:15) In a period of history characterized by a great preoccupation with the future, the observance of this futurological norm is of crucial importance in working out a credible theological perspective. "The Christian gospel can expect to get a hearing in modern culture only when it has some important news to bring about our human future, when it is really concerned about the world's tomorrows. If it has nothing to do with the future, it is properly and understandably dismissed as irrelevant." [9]

For a theology to be both Christian and credible in our day, it must constantly move back and forth between these three horizons of interpretation. Its task is to show how the symbols drawn from our Christian past light up the ambiguous stuff of our contemporary existence and provide clues and pointers to the future for which we hope. An authentic interpretation of Christian faith will, as Harvey Cox has reminded us, "toast *all* the daughters of time." [10] Failing in this, theology develops a dangerous form of tunnel vision which blocks out some of the essential horizons of Christian faith. Theological perspectives become warped and distorted to the extent to which they concentrate too exclusively on one or other of the

[8] Jürgen Moltmann, *Theology of Hope* (New York: Harper & Row, 1967), pp. 35-36.
[9] Carl E. Braaten, *The Future of God* (New York: Harper & Row, 1969), p. 26.
[10] *The Feast of Fools* (Cambridge: Harvard University Press, 1969), p. 42.

norms we have described. In the process, they lose the creative tension between continuity and change which is so indispensable to their Christian credibility.

Let me illustrate. An overemphasis on historical norms can betray theology into a bias toward the past with an accompanying distrust and suspicion of the present and future. The result is some form of biblicism or traditionalism which fails to establish any meaningful contact with contemporary social or cultural movements or provide any significant motive power for shaping the emerging future. A one-sided emphasis on existential-experiential norms can lead to the subservience of theology to the moods and fashions of the prevailing culture. It is productive of an uncritical kind of presentism which lacks a sufficiently transcendent vision to bring the status quo under judgment. Too exclusive a reliance on futurological norms makes theology the ally of a revolutionary fanaticism whose all-consuming passion for the future sweeps away all the values and symbols which history has produced up until the present time. Because of its contempt for the past, and its impatience with the present, this kind of radical futurism is as incapable of comprehending the full sweep of God's historical action as traditionalism and presentism.

To try to forge a unified Christian vision of reality out of the tensions between these three norms is the continuing task of theology. It is an assignment which is perennially inconclusive, and one which is full of risk and uncertainty. We can never be sure that our theological formulations faithfully reproduce the essential Christian message. In fact, there is no simple continuity which can be established with the originative events and convictions of the Christian community. The Christian revelation is inevitably refracted through the prism of history, and changing historical conditions and cultural styles demand its constant reinterpretation and recasting in new language and new symbols.[11]

It is a delusion, therefore, to assume that we can establish continuity with our Christian past, and thereby recapture the normative substance of our faith, simply by repeating biblical or traditional language. The original intentionality of that language may not get communicated at all when it is repeated verbatim in a drastically changed social and cultural situation. Indeed, as John Dillenberger has reminded us, "there are times in history when the repetition of the past actually produces its spiritual and theological opposites, when shifting cultural styles dictate that repetition is not really repeating the past at all." [12]

In some areas, this fact is tacitly accepted by even the most ardent defenders of orthodoxy. Kyle Haselden draws attention to this curious anomaly when he declares that "a biblical literalism that allows no deviation from Scripture is inevitably heretical, a fact acknowledged by fundamentalists when they ignore Paul's plain injunction

[11] Cf. *ibid.*, p. 133. In this work Harvey Cox has proposed what he calls a method of juxtaposition for dealing theologically with the three dimensions of time. His method accents the discontinuity rather than the continuity between past, present, and future as a way of provoking new perceptions and insights. "Traditional theologies emphasize faith's dependence on the past; they are historical. Radical theology, the 'theology of creative negation,' focuses on the present crisis of faith; it is incarnational. Theology of hope is oriented toward the future; it is eschatological. A theology of juxtaposition plays off the tensions among these three not by neatly balancing them but by maximizing the creative friction among all three. . . . Calculated discontinuity exploits the friction between the past and the present to generate new possibilities for the future."

[12] *Contours of Faith* (Nashville: Abingdon Press, 1969), p. 8. Cf. also James M. Robinson, "Hermeneutical Theology" in *The Christian Century,* May 4, 1966, p. 579. "Sometimes a preference for traditional Christian language has been based on the comfortable self-deception that when the right language is used the right subject-matter will somehow be heard. . . . In our situation what happens when traditional Christian language is used is often simply not Christian."

against women speaking in church." [13] At other points, the concern for orthodoxy has, in fact, grievously distorted Christian truth by absolutizing historically conditioned ways of speaking enshrined in biblical and creedal statements. For one example, Paul's admonition in Romans 13 to be subject to the higher powers has been often used by the church as a rationale for social and political conservatism and an uncritical obeisance to secular government, in utter disregard of the radical changes in sociopolitical conditions which have occurred since Paul's day which call for quite different Christian responses. Another example comes from the history of the doctrine of the Trinity. When the formula "three persons in one" was proposed as a way of speaking about God, it was intended as an affirmation of the oneness of God in the face of emerging heretical notions about the deity which moved in the direction of polytheism. Today, the term "person" means something quite different than it did then, and when used in connection with the Trinity, it suggests the very polytheistic notions which the original doctrine was designed to overcome.

Such examples, which could be multiplied endlessly, should make it abundantly clear that deviation from the traditional formulations of the past—its creeds, doctrines and moral codes—is not an act of faithless subversion, but the only way we can honor the real intentions which lay behind them in the beginning. It is not simply that in their original form they are unintelligible and incredible to the contemporary mind; more fundamentally it is the case that the repetition of the original formulations in a quite different historical setting confuses and distorts the very truth that they were intended to convey. It is an irony of history that it is precisely the radicals who often turn out

[13] *Flux and Fidelity* (Richmond: John Knox Press, 1968), p. 59.

to be the most authentic conservatives. Since the Gospel must be carried from one generation to another in the "earthen vessels" of words and ideas and symbols which suffer from the ravages of time, it is best served by those with the courage to construct new and better vehicles of understanding for the purpose of bearing its treasure into a radically new age. Christian credibility can be restored to the church's beliefs only when it is prepared to take the risk of experimenting with new theological constructions which bring together in fresh combinations the new and the old, permanence and novelty, fixity and fluidity, continuity and change.

The Seduction of Verbalism and the Quest for Concreteness

The refusal to risk fresh reinterpretations of basic Christian beliefs usually goes hand in hand with the tendency to succumb to the seductions of an excessive verbalization of faith. A Dutch sociologist, Paul Kraemer, has made a strong indictment of churchmen at this very point: "Just as their ancient predecessors, the medicine-men or shamans in primitive religion, the theologians and clerical leaders of our day seem to have a strong belief in the magical force of sheer verbal repetition." [14]

We are living in a day when it is perilous to place too much confidence in the power of the spoken or written word to convince and persuade. Ours is a "postliterate" age in which men have been surfeited with torrents of words from the advertiser and the political propagandist, words which as frequently as not have lost their credibility by being divorced from appropriate related acts. Bonhoeffer

---

[14] Quoted in Colin W. Williams, *What in the World?* (New York: National Council of Churches in the U.S.A., 1964), p. 71.

was one of those who believed strongly that the church's witness to the world of our day cannot be made persuasive and convincing on the level of verbal communication alone. "The time when men could be told everything by means of words, whether theological or simply pious, is over." [15]

In the wake of the riots in the Watts area of Los Angeles, a young black man poured out the bitterness of his soul to a minister who engaged him in conversation. He told how the police had continued to beat him on the head after they had handcuffed him. In a torrent of resentful words, he talked of the hypocrisy of church people who profess to believe in the Bible but who do nothing about practicing it in their relationships with their fellowmen of another race. One of his outbursts was particularly haunting: "Nobody," he cried, "can define love to me." [16] Of course not! What he desperately wanted to see—and what the world should expect to see—from the church is *not a definition but a demonstration*. Not mere theological abstractions and verbalizations about the meaning of love and brotherhood, but love enacted and incarnate through the presence of the gracious neighbor on the street corners and in the ghettos of our cities!

If God is dead in the consciousness of our culture, it may be because we have talked so incessantly about him in what Kierkegaard called "perpetual Sunday twaddle," in multitudes of words which have had little of the bite of reality about them because they corresponded to nothing in the real world in which we live out our lives. This, of course, is the essence of profanity—taking the Lord's name in vain. And I have no doubt that this kind of profanity— the sort of vacuous verbalization about God of which we

[15] Dietrich Bonhoeffer, *Prisoner for God* (New York: The Macmillan Co., 1953), p. 122.

[16] Quoted in Malcolm Boyd, "Maintaining Humanness in the Freedom Movement" in *Christianity and Crisis*, October 4, 1965, p. 201.

are so often guilty in the church—has contributed enormously to the climate of contemporary unbelief.

We need to be reminded that, as far as our history is concerned, the Gospel was an Act before it became a Word: "The Word was made flesh and dwelt among us (and we beheld his glory, the glory of the only begotten of the Father) full of grace and truth." (John 1:14) A theology which takes this event-character of the Gospel seriously will not rest content with the abstractions of mere *words*, but will press on to show how these words are related to ever fresh incarnations of *word-events* which witness to the healing and reconciling power of God's saving action in Jesus Christ.

Among the many influential theologians of our day who have shared a concern for the lost power of Christian words and symbols is Paul Tillich. In one of his characteristically eloquent sermons he speaks of the current crisis of our religious language and the drastic measures necessary in dealing with it:

The words which are most used in religion are also those whose genuine meaning is almost completely lost and whose impact on the human mind is nearly negligible. Such words must be reborn, if possible; and thrown away if this is not possible, even if they are protected by a long tradition. But there is only one way to re-establish their original meaning and power, namely, to ask ourselves what these words mean for our lives; to ask whether or not they are able to communicate something infinitely important to us.[17]

The restoration of the waning power of Christian words calls for a renewed quest for concreteness in our theological language. Our beliefs must be articulated in such

[17] *The Eternal Now* (New York: Charles Scribner's Sons, 1956), pp. 112-13.

a way that they make unmistakable the vital connections between the ultimate mystery with which we have to do and the concrete realities of our personal and social existence which we confront daily. When we fail to forge these concrete links with our experience, the inevitable result is, as Gordon Kaufman has observed, "a kind of theological inflation, where traditional terms and doctrines appear in great profusion, but what they refer to or count for in the actual stuff of life is less and less evident—the theological language becomes abstract and empty." [18]

If theology is to avoid this semantic inflationary spiral, if it is to deal in a currency which is at all credible and convertible, it must learn to be much more situational in its methodology than has generally been the case. It must abjure the temptation to think of itself as a self-contained intellectual discipline quarantined from the life-and-death issues of our common life. "Theology is not," James H. Cone writes, "an intellectual exercise but a worldly risk." [19] It is the activity of a community of faith which aims to clarify the meaning of that community's involvements in the liberating, humanizing work of God in the world. When it engages in biblical exegesis or historical or systematic studies, it will do so, not for their own sake, but for the sake of giving concrete direction to the church's worldly mission.

The role of the ivory-tower systematizer in theology is increasingly suspect today. Indeed, more and more people are beginning to question whether systematic theology as traditionally pursued is any longer a viable discipline. Certainly, as an enterprise which prepackages a body of truths which are only subsequently related to concrete human struggles and dilemmas, it makes little sense. Vital

[18] *Systematic Theology,* p. 74.
[19] *Black Theology and Black Power* (New York: Seabury Press, 1969), p. 84.

theological insight does not come simply by consulting and reflecting upon the traditions of faith. It is forged out of firsthand participation in the agony and the ecstasy of the human struggle and the attempt to shape the direction of that struggle with the aid of the wisdom, healing, and promise of the Gospel. "The church ought not first decide what its faith is, then retain agencies of communication to promote that faith. An historically sensitive church will allow its conception of the faith to be held in suspension to the world's response—on the mission field, in the schools, in the social structure, from the pulpit, and in the counseling office." [20] To put it another way, it is only out of the context of faithful action and responsible involvement that the authentic contours of the Christian faith begin to come clear.

When theology is practiced in this way as "reflection in action," its language loses its abstractness. Its concepts become less and less purely theoretical and more and more functional and operational in their basic thrust. They serve as tools of personal and social transformation rather than simply theoretical structures of interpretation and explanation. To the degree to which theology shifts its focus from theoretical to actional categories, it becomes less vulnerable to the celebrated criticism of Karl Marx against those who are content to interpret the world without changing it. Insofar as theology is still properly concerned with theory, it takes the form of a theory of Christian practice and mission. Its job is to point out the signs of God's presence in the many concrete contexts in which the struggle for human liberation and maturity is taking place and trace the lineaments of Christian obedience in the midst of that struggle.

In the last few years a great variety of contextual theo-

[20] Carl Michalson, *Worldly Theology: The Hermeneutical Focus of an Historical Faith* (New York: Charles Scribner's Sons, 1967), p. 225.

logical efforts have appeared on the scene—black theology, urban theology, political theology, theology of revolution, theology of secularization—all reflecting the responsible involvements of Christians as agents of redemptive change in society. Theologians have discovered recently that there is a great deal of theology to be learned on a picket line, or at a peace rally, or in the midst of an antipoverty program. Wherever new challenges emerge to test the relevance and power of the Christian faith, there is the opportunity for fresh theological perspectives and understandings to come to birth. Conversely, wherever the Christian faith is applied contextually to emerging issues and problems, it becomes a catalytic agent of social change by motivating and clarifying Christian action and decision-making. When the faith of the church no longer serves as a stimulant for constructive change, when it loses its leverage on the concrete issues which affect the health of the body politic, it is rightly dismissed as innocuous and irrelevant.

Credibility, Conviction, and Commitment

In a recent pioneer study in Black Theology, James H. Cone has delivered himself of some words calculated to jar the equanimity of dispassionate theologians who pride themselves on their scholarly calm and objectivity. "It may be," he writes, "that the importance of any study in the area of morality or religion is determined in part by the emotion expressed. It seems that one weakness of most theological works is their 'coolness' in the investigation of an idea." "Is it not time," he asks provocatively, "for theologians to get upset?" [21]

This is a timely reminder that too little attention has

[21] *Black Theology and Black Power*, p. 3.

been paid to the role of emotion in the formulation and communication of theological beliefs. If such beliefs are to be living convictions, they must have the capacity not only to persuade the mind but to stir the heart. Credibility does not attach itself to our theological ideas simply because they may enjoy the support of objective evidence and scholarly argumentation. It is the mark, rather, of those profound convictions which are affirmed and sustained by the emotional depths of our nature as well as our intellectual judgments. David E. Roberts has some illuminating things to say on this score from the standpoint of psychological wisdom: "Our emotions can *prevent* us from grasping truths which we have the intellectual capacity to understand and accept; but they can also *implement* our search for truth and our willingness to act in the light of it. Where questions of value are involved, the most consistent theory imaginable is impotent unless people believe it with their hearts as well as their heads." As far as the psychology of religious beliefs is concerned, Roberts concludes, "if a person's beliefs are sterile and rigid the explanation may be that they have been robbed of the support of his feelings." [22]

If this is true, we may hypothesize that the reason for much of the sterility of contemporary Christian belief stems from the blocking off of conscious beliefs from the nurturing support of vital subconscious energies which are channeled through the emotions. The traditional Christian symbols and images seem to have lost the capacity to release these powerful energies in the service of a life of faith and Christian commitment. One reason may be that they were born out of an historical situation so alien to the experience of our own culture

[22] *Psychotherapy and the Christian View of Man* (New York: Charles Scribner's Sons, 1950), pp. 58, 60.

that they no longer seem able to express and interpret our kinds of sensibilities, concerns, and commitments.

I am not convinced, however, that the symbolic power of Christian imagery and truth has petered out beyond any hope of revival. In what direction, then, can we look for its rehabilitation?

Samuel H. Miller has expressed the somewhat wistful hope that it might come about through a renewal of the integrity of worship:

If the dead, smothering blubber of respectability could be sloughed off it, if it could once again stand the naked soul before God, if the rushing torrents of man's sins and doubts could pour through his broken prayers, if a new honesty like a strong antiseptic could bathe away the suppurating sores of pious vanity and ecclesiastical foppery—in such worship of such men, human at every level, the image they have adored might come to life again and clutch their souls with eternal mercy.[23]

I am inclined to believe, however, that the compelling power of Christian symbols will be reborn on the streets before it is revived in the sanctuary. For only in the context of a radical kind of life-commitment which pushes us out onto the raw and bleeding frontiers of life in the world will the symbols of a cross and a resurrection begin to grip us again with elemental power. Perhaps when we begin to make ourselves vulnerable to the sufferings of men, taste the bitter dregs of human alienation, and put our bodies on the line for the poor and the dispossessed, the Christ-image will begin to glow again with a fresh credibility. As a matter of fact, our recent experience has provided us with some models as to how this might happen. In the courageous witness of a Martin Luther King,

[23] *The Dilemma of Modern Belief* (New York: Harper & Row, 1963), pp. 35-36.

a Father Groppi, and the brothers Berrigan the guts of the gospel has been again finding a living and convincing embodiment. Such men are exemplary incarnations of an axiom once laid down by H. H. Farmer: "The Christian affirmation about Christ can only become a living and massive conviction within the soul in the course of a life of Christian discipleship itself." [24] Perhaps it is still true that "the blood of the martyrs is the seed of the church."

At a very fundamental level, the problem of theological credibility comes down to the question of the quality of our commitments. Warren Lane Molton dares to embarrass us by asking: "What is anyone doing that demands God? When will life be either so celebrative or so treacherous as to need gospel? What is sacrifice in this particular time of life-loving?" [25] Not until the church faces up realistically to those kinds of searching questions, will it stand a chance of closing the credibility gap in its theology as well as in its life. When our commitments move beyond the level of conventional expectations and begin to embrace the revolutionary imperative, we will not have to worry about sagging beliefs and dusty symbols. For then the flame of conviction will begin to ignite the imagery and conceptuality of faith and, without artificial contrivance, the spontaneous combustion of an "ultimate concern" will begin to create and re-create living symbols adequate for its expression.

Credibility and Consistency

The explorations in contemporary belief on which we are about to launch in succeeding chapters are selective probes

[24] Quoted by F. G. Healey in *Prospects for Theology* (Digswell Place: James Nisbet & Co., 1966), p. 9.
[25] "The Church as Servant-Critic to Revolution" in *Central Baptist Seminary Journal*, October, 1969, p. 9.

into some of the more basic themes of Christian theology. They represent a search for a core of credible meaning to sustain our Christian action and reflection in a revolutionary age. They make no claim to be a comprehensive survey of Christian beliefs. The attempt to apply as rigorously as possible the tests of credibility implied in the foregoing discussion has prompted us to circumvent certain areas of theological investigation which have figured importantly in classical theology. We have sought to accentuate those strands of the Christian tradition which hold the most promise for weaving together a viable faith-perspective for the contemporary Christian in mission.

We have endeavored, however, to provide something more than a potpourri of unrelated and fragmentary insights. One of the criteria of credibility must surely be a reasonable amount of consistency. Without some kind of inner coherence, no theological position can provide the unity of vision which enables truth to shine in its own light and impress itself upon us as inherently credible.

We must face the fact, of course, that we live in an age in which the seamless robe of Christian tradition has been rent asunder. The radical fragmentation and pluralization of our culture creates enormous difficulties for projecting a unitary vision of Christian truth and reality. All attempts at restoring the fabric of faith in our time must appear at best as modest patchwork efforts when compared with the great systems of the past. Paul Tillich was doubtless the last great systematician in theology whom we shall see for a long time. At this point in history, the interests of Christian credibility will not be served by trying to press the data of Christian experience and thought into the Procrustean bed of some grand overarching system. Inevitably we find ourselves resonating to some notes of the Gospel more than to others. This does not absolve us, however, of the obligation to try to explicate the wholeness of the Gospel as we explore as faithfully as possible the "many-sided wisdom of God." But the unity for which we are searching is not the static unity of a set of abstract, logically interlocking, rational principles. It is the dynamic unity of a faith-stance which struggles to make sense of the anguish and aspirations of contemporary man in the light of God's liberating action in Jesus Christ.

Undue deference to contemporary sensibilities can betray theology into sacrificing the minimal coherence with which we can alone make sense of the Christian faith on its own terms. The weakness of the "death of God" theology, in its response to the crisis of theological meaning in our day, lies at this point. It has sought to reduce the entire Christian language-game to talk about man and his possibilities of freedom. In an attempt to preserve a meaningful link with the Christian tradition, it has continued also to talk about Jesus as the paradigm of human freedom. In doing so, however, it has been inconsistent. For, in giving to Jesus their unconditional allegiance, radical theologians, in effect, treat him as God.[26] Martin E. Marty has summed up very succinctly the resultant dilemma: "Human freedom-talk without Jesus-talk is unsatisfying and cannot be considered Christian. Jesus-talk without God-talk is idolatrous. Yet God-talk is problematic." [27] This episode illustrates, not only the mutual interdependence of basic Christian affirmations, but the difficulties which attend all reductionist theologies which, in their rightful concern for credibility, try to dispense with some of the key terms of the Christian equation.

However problematic, we will begin our study by diving immediately into the murky waters of an exploration into

[26] For an excellent critique of the death of God theologians on this point, see Thomas W. Ogletree, *The Death of God Controversy* (Nashville: Abingdon Press, 1966), pp. 42 ff.

[27] Robert L. Richard, *Secularization Theology* (New York: Herder and Herder, 1967), p. x.

the reality of God. We can expect those waters to come clear, however, only as our God-talk is informed throughout by Jesus-talk and man-talk: only as the activity of God is seen as focused in the person and mission of Jesus, and in relation to the problematic of man's personal and social existence. We will assume that the credibility of belief in God can be established only by showing how that belief is relevant to man's quest for his authentic humanity, and how it finds its confirmation in the appearance of the new humanity in Jesus Christ as the prefiguration of our own future.

Additionally, our Christian affirmations concerning a living God must gain their credibility through a Christian life-style which involves an authentically new way of being human, and a church which is clear about its role as the vanguard of the redeeming and humanizing mission of God in the world. Only a radical rediscovery by the church of its revolutionary mission can unlock the healing insights of the Gospel and unleash its transforming power to liberate men for new possibilities of existence.

Finally, a truly convincing interpretation of the Christian faith for our future-oriented age must take the form of a theology of hope. It must provide a structure of belief which specifies the ground and goal of our hope for the future, and a dynamism for ongoing revolutionary change by which the dehumanizing and destructive elements of the status quo are constantly challenged.

Our search for Christian credibility must assay the task, then, of weaving these interrelated theological concerns into a single working perspective of faith. Its success or failure depends on its ability to provide a meaningful horizon of understanding which clarifies our confusions, illumines our intellectual and spiritual darkness, and moves us into creative and militant participation in God's mission of renewal in the world.

PART TWO

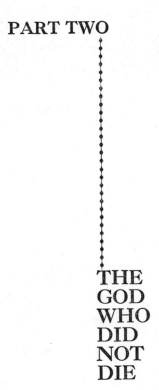

THE
GOD
WHO
DID
NOT
DIE

II

EXPLORING
THE MYSTERY OF GOD

There is no point of Christian doctrine which causes more perplexity and confusion today than the most fundamental of all affirmations which Christians make—their belief in God. If there is a crisis of credibility in contemporary theology, it centers around this basic Christian tenet. "One of the most obvious conclusions to be drawn from the latest developments in Protestant theology," writes Schubert Ogden, "is that the reality of God has now become the central theological problem." [1]

If the reality of God has become problematic for the professional theologian, it is also true that the typical man on the street shares in his problem. The fact that some theologians have in our day been seriously raising the question as to whether God is dead or alive reflects the puzzlement and difficulty that increasing numbers of people are having with the whole notion of God. I suspect, if they are honest, few people today find it easy to sustain a meaningful faith in a living God. When Christopher Fry, in *A Sleep of Prisoners,* has David say to Adams, "Allow me to make the introduction. God, man. Man, God," Adams' poignant rejoinder rings a bell with most of us: "I wish it could be so easy." [2] The fact is that it is getting harder all the time for people in our day to affirm a belief in a God whom they know to be alive. If there was a day when God's presence was luminous in their lives, that day is no more. For many of us, Job articulates our experience

---

[1] *The Reality of God* (New York: Harper & Row, 1966), p. 1.
[2] (London: Oxford University Press, 1951), p. 12.

better than anyone else. "Behold, I go forward but He is not there; and backward, but I cannot perceive Him. On the left hand, where He doth work, but I cannot behold Him. He hideth Himself on the right hand that I cannot see Him." (Job 23:8-9)

The Death-of-God Mood

I am suggesting that there is something that might be called a "death-of-God" mood abroad in the world today—a *Zeitgeist* which the church must learn to understand and come to terms with, if there is to be any hope of finding a cure for the malaise into which faith has fallen. It cannot afford the luxury of a defensive and emotional denunciation of the death-of-God theologians as subverters of the faith. If we are to have any success in rehabilitating the credibility of belief in God, we must seek to understand the reasons for the mood to which the death-of-God theology has attempted, however inadequately, to respond.

I must confess that I find very unsatisfying some of the extreme explanations of this mood suggested by the radical theologians: for example, that the death of God is a real event, datable in time; that there was a time when there existed a primordial, transcendent God, but now he is dead; that the meaning of the Incarnation is that God, in a supreme act of self-emptying, died in Jesus; that is, in Jesus he became wholly immanent in history, and died as a being who transcends history. For these men, the loss of faith in our day is to be explained by an actual historical event in which the God of the Christian tradition, who once was alive, has ceased to exist.[3]

[3] Of ten possible meanings of the phrase "death of God" delineated by Altizer and Hamilton, they identify the following as the one which characterizes the position of radical theology: "That there once was a God to whom adoration, praise and trust were appropriate, possible, and

I propose to try to make sense of the phrase "death of God" by regarding it as a vivid metaphor to describe three more or less related things that have been happening to us in our modern world that have made it increasingly difficult for us to affirm a faith in a living God. These three developments are: 1) the erosion of faith in God by the acids of modern secularism; 2) the perpetuation of outmoded conceptualizations of God which modern man finds increasingly incredible; and 3) the trivialization of belief in God by a false spiritualization of his activity.

The Acids of Secularism

Particularly since the eighteenth century, our modern culture has been undergoing a radical process of secularization. Under the aegis of science and technology, more and more areas of life have moved out from under religious tutelage and established their autonomy. This emancipation has unfortunately been accompanied by the increasing dominance of a secularistic ideology—a way of thinking for which only objective, scientifically observable and verifiable things are real. The assumption of the modern secularist is that, if God is real, he must somehow be an object like a germ or a grasshopper, a planet or a spaceship. These things we are able to talk about meaningfully in sentences which are capable of being verified or falsified by an appeal to appropriate public evidence. This is not true, however, we are reminded, in the case of God. You will look in vain for any empirical evidence to show whether the statement "God exists" is true or false. This means that, when I use the word "God," I am making

---

even necessary, but that now there is no such God." T. J. J. Altizer and William Hamilton, *Radical Theology and the Death of God* (Indianapolis: Bobbs-Merrill, 1966), p. x.

meaningless noises, for I am using a word which refers to nothing in the real world.

One of the radical theologians, Paul van Buren, insists that it is this empirical or scientific way of looking at things (which demands that all statements of truth be capable of being verified by objective evidence) which makes it impossible for a truly twentieth-century man to find meaning any longer in talk about God. "The empiricist in us," he says, "finds the heart of the difficulty not in what is said about God, but in the very talking about God at all. We do not know 'what' God is, and we cannot understand how the word 'God' is being used." [4] Actually, for men like van Buren, it is just as nonsensical to say that God is dead as it is to say he is alive, for the very word "God" is a meaningless blank which cannot be shown to refer to anything at all in the only world which they are prepared to accept as real in a scientific age. Strictly speaking, then, "the problem now is that the word 'God' is dead."

I would like to argue that it is possible to be a truly secular man in tune with the scientific temper of our times without drawing this conclusion. Here we have to distinguish carefully between a true secularity and a false secularism. A true secularity will agree that, when it comes to germs and grasshoppers, planets and spaceships, the only legitimate kind of knowledge there is, is scientific knowledge, based on such things as observation, experiment, and verification. Into this realm of finite things and objects and their relationships, religion or theology has no business intruding. Here science has the last word. At this level there is no need to bring God in to fill up the gaps of our ignorance. The scientist has no need to go to the book of Genesis for information as to how the world came into being. La Place was right when he said: "God! I have

---

[4] *The Secular Meaning of the Gospel* (New York: The Macmillan Co., 1963), p. 84.

no need of that hypothesis." We can indeed be grateful that, in this sense, modern man has come of age and that, as Bonhoeffer put it so strikingly, God has been teaching man how to get along without him. This kind of secularity is thus a mark of man's maturity which Christians should applaud.

It is one thing, however, to say that science is completely competent to know whatever can be known about the finite forces of nature and man's social environment. It is quite another thing to say that this is the only kind of knowledge there is—and that, if the reality Christians call God cannot be known through methods akin to those which science uses, he cannot be real after all. This is the false conclusion of a dogmatic secularism which illicitly attempts to understand all of reality in terms of the paradigm provided by the objectifying methods of science. It represents, moreover, the intuitive, often unarticulated, assumption of many in our culture who have been mesmerized by the spectacular successes and enormous prestige of science into concluding that it alone is a valid and credible authority for modern man. In subsequent discussion, we shall hope to be able to show that our secular experience itself yields intimations of a dimension of reality which can be appropriately symbolized only by the notion of God.

Outmoded Conceptualizations of God

Unfortunately, the secularistic denial of the reality of God has been aided and abetted by inadequate ideas of God to which we have clung in the church, and which thoughtful people are finding more and more difficult to accept as meaningful. Thus the false secularization of which I have been speaking has been made almost inevitable by an erroneous, and for most modern men, incredible conceptualization of God. According to this conceptualization,

45

God has been thought of as a being separate from other beings, occupying a supernatural realm above and beyond this world, from which he descends from time to time to direct and control events in accordance with his purposes. God is imagined in mythological terms as existing "up there." Or the more sophisticated may conceive him in metaphysical terms as "out there." [5] If he is no longer portrayed as an oversized man with a beard, at least he is regarded as a being which can be located in the space-time continuum. He is thus part of the whole of reality, even though its most important part, a being alongside other beings, even though he is the Supreme Being.

It was this supernaturalistic notion of God which the Russian cosmonaut, Yuri Gagarin, had in mind when, returning from his space journey, he ridiculed the idea of God by saying that he had looked everywhere in space and was unable to find God anywhere. Of course, it may be objected that this is a caricature of God as Christians today understand him. Indeed it is, but it is surprising how many people still entertain such ideas. I can recall a student in one of my classes who insisted that, if our spaceships probed far enough into space, it should be possible for them one day to locate the place we call heaven. And presumably God would be there! Such experiences confirm for me the truth of Bishop Robinson's observation "that many popular religious ideas are still incredibly more naive than bishops and clergy often suppose." [6]

Such ideas of God make atheism easy, and in the age in which we live, well nigh inevitable. Once we bring God

----

[5] Cf. John A. T. Robinson, *Honest to God* (Philadelphia: Westminster Press, 1963). "In place of a God who is literally or physically 'up there' we have accepted, as part of our mental furniture, a God who is spiritually or metaphysically 'out there.'" (P. 13)

[6] David L. Edwards, ed. *The Honest to God Debate* (Philadelphia: Westminster Press, 1963), p. 257.

down to the level of planets and spaceships, our secularist friend is entitled to ask: "Where is the scientific evidence for this being which you call 'God'?" Paul Tillich was undoubtedly right when he said: "In making God an object besides other objects, the existence and nature of which are matters of argument, theology supports the escape to atheism. The first step to atheism is always a theology which drags God down to the level of doubtful things. The game of the atheist is then very easy. For he is perfectly justified in destroying such a phantom and all its ghostly qualities." [7]

But, it may be asked, does not the Bible present us with some such picture of God as this—a God who is a personal being, who created the world by a fiat of his Word, who converses with men either directly or through angelic messengers, who breaks into their history in miraculous revelations and mighty works, who sent his Son down from his celestial abode and receives him back again to be seated at his right hand, and who will at the end of history gather all men before his judgment seat to separate the faithful from the wicked?

This is indeed the way in which the Bible pictures God. The question we must raise, however, is whether it is necessary to take these pictures literally in order to preserve a truly Christian understanding of God. If it is, I suspect that fewer and fewer will be able to call themselves Christians in our day. For such naively supernaturalistic representations of God are simply no longer credible to increasing numbers of thoughtful people.

Recent theologians have been making it easier for us to make sense of these biblical pictures, not as literal representations of God in terms of a magnified human being,

[7] *The Shaking of the Foundations* (New York: Charles Scribner's Sons, 1948), p. 45.

but as symbolic and mythical characterizations of God as the ultimate reality which is the source and ground and goal of our lives and of our world. It was necessary for the writers of the Bible, as it is necessary for us, to talk about God in concrete images and symbols drawn from our human experience, for these are the only ones we have. The biblical writers used images that were consistent with the worldview that prevailed in their day which thought in terms of a three-decker universe, with heaven above and hell beneath and the earth in between, and man being controlled by good and evil supernatural powers emanating from above and below. This view of the world and God was highly mythical, representing God objectively as a localized being who moves among men as if he were one of them.

The danger of taking this picture-thinking about God literally is that it reduces him, in effect, to a finite being. As Tillich says, it "deprives God of his ultimacy and religiously speaking, of his majesty. It draws him down to the level of that which is not ultimate, the finite and conditional." [8] This is to fall into what the Bible calls idolatry —the identification of what has no rightful claim to ultimacy with the ultimate reality itself. This, even more than the strain that it puts on our credibility, is the weakness and danger of traditional supernaturalism.

In the remainder of this chapter and the next, we shall attempt to work out a conceptualization of God which avoids the problems that supernaturalism inherited in interpreting too literally the objectifying, mythical representations of God in the Bible. Unless such experiments in reinterpretation are vigorously pursued in our day, we can expect the acids of secularism to continue to eat away at the vitals of contemporary faith. For, as Samuel H. Miller has correctly observed, "atheism usually appears in

[8] *Dynamics of Faith,* p. 52.

the world as the void left by inadequate representations of God." [9]

The Heresy of Spiritualization

Perhaps even more damaging to the integrity of faith today than obsolete ideas of God is the distortion of understanding which occurs when we spiritualize away his activity in history. On this point, the judgment of Harvey Cox is a sound one: "The spiritualizers always try to banish God from the earth and to distort the pictures of how he gets his work done in his world. Spiritualization is the characteristic heresy of the twentieth century, especially among American Protestants." [10] There is a widespread tendency in the church to so spiritualize our talk about God that he has little or nothing to do with the concrete realities of our life in the world, nor does he affect in any significant way the nature of our worldly commitments.

Werner Pelz has made the point in this way: "When we use the word 'God' we are talking about something which no longer connects with anything in most people's life, except with whatever happens to be left over after the vital connections have been made." [11] As someone has said in a facetious vein—the problem today is not so much that God is dead, but that he is unemployed! Or, to put it another way, it is not that he is dead; he has been reported as "missing in action."

Paradoxically, the very effort to protect the reality of God by restricting him to the safety of the so-called

[9] *The Dilemma of Modern Belief*, p. 45.
[10] *God's Revolution and Man's Responsibility* (Valley Forge: Judson Press, 1965), p. 28.
[11] Quoted by J. A. T. Robinson, *The New Reformation?* (Philadelphia: Westminster Press, 1965), p. 109.

"spiritual realm," can lead to the triumph of secularism. A leading German theologian, Gerhard Ebeling, has warned us of the way in which a false spiritualization of our talk about God can lead to the wrong kind of world-liness and godlessness:

Christianity is constantly in danger of becoming pagan precisely where it seeks to be most pious. . . . The spiritual realm is then made into a world of its own, a separate reality which passes by the world as it really is, instead of engaging it. . . . Could it be that separatist, unworldly talk of God which builds a world apart is likewise worldly talk of God in that negative, basically godless sense? It is indeed! The extreme possibilities of sepa-ration join hands: atheistic and, as it were, purely religious, pure-ly spiritual talk of God. Both leave the world without God and God without the world.[12]

If we are going to combat successfully the death of God mood abroad today, we are going to have to learn to think and speak of God in worldly terms. The God of the Chris-tian faith is, if I may say so, a very worldly God! He is the Lord of history who spoke to his people of old through the secular events of an exodus, an exile, and an unbeliev-ing tyrant called Cyrus, and who in the fullness of time manifested himself in the fleshly reality of a real person called Jesus of Nazareth. If we are to meet him today, it will not be in some otherworldly spiritual retreat, some-where on the outer fringes of life, but in the depths of our this-worldly existence, as life pulls us up short with its demands for truth and love, integrity and accountability, and forces upon us the question of its ultimate meaning and purpose. As Thomas Ogletree has written, "reflection on the meaning of God must take its starting point in those explosive happenings in the midst of life which empower

[12] *Word and Faith* (Philadelphia: Fortress Press, 1963), p. 358.

man for responsible action, which open up new possibilities for the actualization of a more human future." [13]

The Abuse of God-Talk

While we may conclude that the publication of God's obituary has been a trifle premature, there should be no minimizing the notorious difficulties that face us as we endeavor to talk about God today in a meaningful way. Part of the problem stems from the fact that in much of its popular usage the name of God has been so debased, cheapened, and prostituted for human ends, that it is no longer capable of evoking a sense of the divine mystery. As a result, we suffer from what Ebeling has aptly described as a kind of "language poisoning." "This is not," he goes on to say, "because God has completely vanished from our language, but because God is festering in our language." [14] Such poisoning of our language concerning God always takes place when we allow it to degenerate into a merely ceremonial way of speaking, or a religious cover-up for all too human purposes.

Roger L. Shinn has drawn our attention to "the kind of heresy that reduces God to a kindly accomplice to our purposes." Illustrative of this heresy is a nationwide advertising campaign launched by the state of Kansas to attract industry. Its claim was that Kansas had long ago developed the "Great Society." And what did that mean? "In Kansas the 'Great Society' means Great People, people who want to work for a living, people who give a day's work for a day's pay, people who believe in God, people

---

[13] "The Shifting Focus of Theological Reflection" in Martin E. Marty and Dean G. Peerman, eds., *New Theology No. 6* (New York: The Macmillan Co., 1969), p. 64.

[14] *God and Word* (Philadelphia: Fortress Press, 1967), p. 2.

who believe in each other, people who believe in free enterprise, people who believe in America." [15]

An even more blatant example of this kind of abuse of God-talk emerged from a recent mayoralty election in Minneapolis. A police detective, just elected mayor on the strength of a hard-line "law and order" campaign, informed his audience at his victory celebration that he was prepared to make his first appointment. "My chief advisor is going to be God," he roared at the startled crowd, "and don't you forget it!"

The outrageous blasphemy of that outburst lies quite simply in its reduction of God-talk to the level of a political slogan. It utterly lacks, as so much of our speaking of God does, any real sense of the uncontrollable, unapproachable, awe-inspiring mystery which is God. All speech about God, if it is to be authentic, must arise out of the experience of being grasped and overwhelmed by a mystery which we cannot manipulate for our own ends. This is the meaning of the commandment: "You shall not take the name of the Lord your God in vain" (Exod. 20:7). It is also, as Tillich has reminded us, the explanation of "the sublime embarrassment that we feel when we say 'God.' " It is the reason why "those of us who are grasped by the mystery present in the name of God are often stung when the name is used in governmental and political speeches, in opening prayers for conferences and dinners, in secular and religious advertisements, and in international war propaganda." [16]

The ancient Hebrews were able to speak about God only with the greatest of reticence. Because the divine name

---

[15] "The Public Responsibility of Theology" in *America and the Future of Theology*, ed. William A. Beardslee (Philadelphia: Westminster Press, 1967), p. 188.

[16] *The Eternal Now*, pp. 93, 96.

symbolized for them an awesome and holy mystery, they frequently avoided the use of that name entirely. The reason for this hesitancy is clear. To name something is to have a measure of control over it. And God for them was that mysterious, transcendent reality which could not be subjected to human control.

Moses learned this lesson well through his encounter with God in his vision of the burning bush. In responding to the divine summons to be the liberator of his people, Moses asks that God identify himself with a name which will authorize and sanction his mission in the eyes of the Israelites. God's answer is simply to say "I am who I am," or, according to another rendering, "I will be what I will be" (Exod. 3:14). In effect, Moses learned that the mysterious, unpredictable reality of God cannot, in the final analysis, be encompassed in speech or captured in a name. No man, therefore, ought to refer to such a God without some sense of embarrassment and inadequacy.

Various and subtle are the ways in which we manage to talk about God without such reticence and embarrassment, all the time profaning his mystery and his majesty. The glibness with which we so often have identified him in practice with our own thoughts, our own beliefs, our own moral scruples, our own selfish ambitions, our own church, our own class, our own race, our own nation, has undoubtedly contributed to God's "death" in our time. Samuel H. Miller (following Nietzsche) has disturbingly indicted us Christians for being parties to the crime of deicide. We have killed God by domesticating him and appointing him to serve our own purposes. "We domesticated God, stripped Him of awe and majesty, trapped Him in nets of ideas . . . , cornered Him ecclesiastically, taught Him our rules and dressed Him in our vanity, and trained

53

Him to acknowledge our tricks and bow to our ceremonial expectations." [17]

James Baldwin, the noted Negro author, though making no pretense at being a theologian, senses the fact that this kind of idolatry, which seeks to subvert the transcendent and imperious mystery of God, is an enemy of the true emancipation of his people. A God whom we can control, and use as a means of controlling others, cannot be a source of genuine liberation. "I suggest that the role of the Negro in American life has something to do with our concept of what God is, and from my point of view, this concept is not big enough. It has got to be made much bigger than it is because God is, after all, not anybody's toy. To be with God is really to be involved with some enormous, overwhelming desire and joy, and power which you cannot control, which controls you. I conceive of my own life as a journey toward something I do not understand, which in the going toward, makes me better." [18]

That very theological statement by a "non-theologian" is clearly echoed in this word from a theologian, Harvey Cox: "Thus we meet God at those places in life where we come up against that which is not pliable and disposable, at those hard edges where we are both stopped and challenged to move ahead. God meets us as the transcendent, at those aspects of our experience which can never be transmuted into extensions of ourselves." [19]

The Agitating Mystery

There at least we have a hint as to where we must begin in recovering the credibility of our talk about God. What-

[17] *The Dilemma of Modern Belief,* pp. 45-46.
[18] *Nobody Knows My Name* (New York: Dell Books, 1961), p. 113.
[19] *The Secular City* (New York: The Macmillan Co., 1965), p. 262.

ever else God is, he is that disturbingly mysterious "Other" who pulls us up short, turns us around in our tracks, and propels us, as in the case of Abraham, on a journey into an open future. "By faith Abraham . . . went out, not knowing where he was to go." (Heb. 11:8) In a suggestive phrase, a German theologian, Herbert Braun, speaks of God as "the Whence of my being agitated," or, translated more literally, "driven around." [20] Must we not say that God is the original "outside agitator"? Acknowledged or not, he is that disturbing presence in men's hearts which goads them into perpetual restlessness and discontent with things as they are. He is the source of the artist's painfully creative vision, the scientist's consuming thirst for knowledge, and the dreams of a more just and human social order which torment the souls of the Martin Luther Kings of our world. He is that transcendent lure which draws all men, and indeed the whole creation, toward their intended wholeness and fulfillment.

The power of this agitating mystery to propel us into new possibilities of life is hampered for many by its imprisonment in static, spatial imagery. If belief in the transcendence of God is to be made credible to men today, its meaning must be sought in those compelling experiences of creativity and grace which arise out of our encounters with the mystery of life itself. William Hordern clarifies our understanding of transcendence at this point: "To say that God is transcendent is not to picture the universe as a spatial box with God overflowing it or standing outside it. It is to point to the mystery of God. The same is true when we speak of God as 'high and lifted up.' (Isa. 6:1) This does not mean that we need a telescope to see God

[20] "The Problem of a New Testament Theology" in Robert M. Funk, ed., *The Bultmann School of Biblical Interpretation: New Directions?* (New York: Harper & Row, 1965), p. 183.

beyond the farthest star; it means that God is the Mysterious One." [21]

To speak of God as a mystery is, in biblical terms, to speak of his holiness. Holiness is the essential quality of deity as deity—that which sets God apart from all created existence. "I am God, not man; the Holy One in the midst of thee." (Hos. 11:9) "For as the heavens are higher than the earth, so are my ways than your ways, and my thoughts than your thoughts." (Isa. 55:9) Because the holiness of God consists of his mysterious "otherness" from man and the world, it points to the unfathomable mystery of his being, without which he would not be God. For this reason the Swedish theologian, Gustav Aulén, insists that "every statement about God . . . ceases to be an affirmation about God when it is not projected against the background of his holiness." [22] To rob God of his holiness, in whatever way, is to deny his reality as God.

The Beyond in the Midst

We must face the fact that in the ears of many people today, however, talk about the holy and the mysterious smacks of the spooky and the occult. It conjures up images of séances and mystic visions—abnormal experiences of which enlightened modern men are inclined to be highly skeptical. It must be made clear that, for the Christian, the mystery of God is met nowhere else than in the normal, ordinary, concrete experiences and relationships of life. As Bonhoeffer liked to put it, "God is the 'beyond' in the midst of our life." [23] The holy is encountered in and

[21] *Speaking of God* (New York: The Macmillan Co., 1964), p. 113.
[22] *The Faith of the Christian Church* (Philadelphia: The Muhlenberg Press, 1948), p. 122.
[23] *Prisoner for God*, p. 124.

through the profane, the sacred in and through the secular, the acts of God in and through natural, worldly events.

This conviction that God is to be found in the secular and worldly, and nowhere else, is rooted firmly in the Christian belief that the divine mystery has become incarnate in history and the infinite power and ground of our being has been revealed in the finite things of this world. In no other way could God speak to us except through our own history. "Were God to speak to us in a non-worldly way," writes Karl Barth, "He would not speak to us at all." [24]

To find God we do not look for supernatural interventions from another world than our own. To come face to face with him we do not "take an elevator to the eternal," as Reinhold Niebuhr used to caution his students. We attend to the intimations of his presence and activity in the historical events which impinge upon us in this world. Ronald Gregor Smith states the matter very perceptively:

A faith which takes us not out of this world, into a sphere of arbitrary interventions, but deeper into the world in its historicity, is, it seems to me, the very crux of our belief in the historical Incarnation. In this historical Word of God we see nothing arbitrary, but the endless pressure of God through the events, the things and the people and the situations of this world. We cannot be in a closer relation to God than the one he himself provides by means of his own modest pressure upon us.[25]

On the basis of the incarnation of God in Christ, Christians affirm that the divine mystery has been revealed concretely and historically under what Luther liked to call the "masks" or "veils" of creaturely existence. Luther was impatient with a "theology of glory" which vainly

---

[24] *Church Dogmatics* (Edinburgh: T. & T. Clark, 1936), I/1, p. 192.
[25] *The Whole Man* (Philadelphia: Westminster Press, 1969), p. 110.

sought by human speculation to mount up to God's level and grasp him directly in his "naked majesty." A more modest "theology of the cross" is content to apprehend the mystery of God where he himself has chosen to disclose it, namely, in those human and worldly media which paradoxically veil and at the same time reveal the divine presence and activity.

This means that, even in his revelation, God remains a mystery. The revealed God is still the hidden God. Now, however, he is a meaningful mystery, worthy of our worship and a credible object of our devotion and allegiance. He is no longer an opaque enigma, requiring the sacrifice of our intellect and leaving our quest for meaning frustrated and unsatisfied. In his incarnate form, he is apprehended as a grace-filled mystery, capable of giving direction and purpose to our lives and bringing them under judgment.

To say, in this way, that God's revelation is always hidden, is to say that it can be recognized and apprehended only through faith. There is nothing so obvious about God's revelatory activity in the world that it can command our assent or provide us with the basis for demonstrative knowledge. If God's actions in history were that public, it is difficult to understand why all men would not be coerced into becoming believers. For "seeing," after all, "is believing."

Faith, however, is not sight. And what can be "seen" of those events through which God is claimed to have revealed himself are, except through the "eyes of faith," perfectly natural phenomena. That is why the majority of Jesus' contemporaries were able to see in him no more than a great moral and religious teacher, or a misguided, troublemaking, eccentric preacher. Even his own disciples were unable to recognize him as the Christ until Peter's confession at Caesarea Philippi; and then, according to

Jesus, it was not "flesh and blood" which revealed this to him, but God himself, enabling him to see something in this very human and historical life which did not "meet the eye" of the public observer. Similarly, faith is able to read the history of Israel as the history of God's redemptive action in the life of a people chosen for a unique mission to mankind. It can just as easily be read by a secular historian as the saga of an obscure band of ancient nomadic tribes struggling to achieve their nationhood.

Discerning the Action of God

The same paradoxical character of God's activity in history can be illustrated in terms of our experience today. The Christian's involvement in the struggle for justice and human dignity, for the eradication of poverty, for the reconciliation of the races, for the building of a peaceful world order, proceeds on the assumption that God is actively at work in those revolutionary changes which are moving in the direction of these objectives. But this is an assumption of faith which cannot be proved. Since the same events are susceptible to other interpretations, the church is inevitably vulnerable to criticism from those who are unable to discern the action of God in the particular social or political activities in which it may be involved.

This is the peculiar pathos which attends the efforts of every church which tries to respond sensitively and faithfully to what it believes to be the action and summons of God in the tumultuous events of its particular time and place in history. The pathos of Christian decision is an inescapable consequence of the paradoxical nature of God's action. That action, as Ronald Gregor Smith reminds us, "unites within itself the ordinary actions of the world with God's loving will for the world." This being

59

the case, "it means that in each event which comes into your life you are invited, or if you like you are challenged, to respond to this event as one in which simultaneously with its everyday meaning you recognize and acknowledge that here God is at work." [26]

There is, in the final analysis, no escaping the risk involved in the assertion that God is at work here or there in the ambiguous events of our world. If we really believe in a living God who is redemptively at work in the daily stuff of human existence and worldly events, we must be prepared to risk concrete judgments as to the direction in which that work is proceeding and the means by which it is being carried out. We must, for example, be ready to hear and identify the voice of God in such events as the anti-Vietnam War protests, the abrasive confrontations of the student militants, the insistent demands of the Black Power movement, the revolution of rising expectations among the poor.

Such judgments will, of course, never be infallible. There is no assurance that we will never be wrong. For this reason, many Christians are immobilized when it comes to relating their faith to complex social issues. Their passion always to be in the right, their insistence on keeping their faith unsullied by uncertainty, inhibits them from ever taking the plunge into the murky waters of involvement in those critical but ambiguous issues with respect to which the very future of humanity hangs in the balance. As a consequence, the application of their faith is restricted to relatively safe judgments having to do with private and familial virtues. Among other things, this is a subtle repudiation of the doctrine of justification by faith. It is an attempt to relate to God on such terms that we will always know we are in the right. It is, as Bonhoeffer points

[26] *The Whole Man,* p. 130.

out, the way of the Pharisee—the man who tries to justify himself by a knowledge of good and evil from which all uncertainty and risk have been removed. The end result is to reject faith in a living God who calls us to join him in risky obedience, where he is at work in the world making "all things new."

It is possible, of course, to exaggerate the element of risk in faith. We hold no brief for Kierkegaard's view of faith as a completely ungrounded leap—a passionate inward adherence to an objective uncertainty which leaves the believer suspended, as it were, "over seventy thousand fathoms of water." To be sure, faith does not equip the Christian with a foolproof radar system by which he can detect the presence and activity of God in the events of history. On the other hand, it is much more than a subjective hunch or a purely arbitrary guess.

Some theologians have described faith as essentially a miraculous and immediate creation of God in the soul of the believer. But such a "tap-on-the-shoulder" notion of faith is bound to be unconvincing to thoughtful men and women today. Faith conceived in this way becomes "an empty abstraction unrelated to all the concrete decisions through which one orders his life." [27] If faith is to be a credible option for modern man, it must be seen as a vital interaction between the self and those concrete realities of history which become luminous and transparent to the divine presence and activity. Faith is a way of seeing "beneath the surface" of ordinary events, a kind of depth discernment of a meaning and significance in those events which escapes the casual and uncommitted observer.

The individual believer does not, of course, start out *de novo* to discern the manifestation of God in the events

---

[27] Kaufman, *Systematic Theology*, p. 304 *n.*

of his life and his world. The Christian belongs to a community of faith which feeds upon a storehouse of memories of revealing events from the past, through which God has made himself known to his people. This memory bank, which has been kept alive for us through the Bible, provides us with normative clues as to how and where we are to look for the disclosure of God in the experiences and events of our lives today. The central clue is Jesus Christ, in whose person and ministry Christians find a unique focusing and a definitive revelation of both the mystery of God's being and activity and the true meaning of our humanity. Thus the living God, whom we may expect to encounter in the events of our own time, is the same God who was the God of Abraham, Isaac, and Jacob, and the God and Father of our Lord Jesus Christ.

If this God to whom the biblical writers bear witness is to become real to us today, however, we must be able to point to those concrete processes, events, and situations in which he is alleged to be at work as a living, dynamic power. Nothing less than a situational theology will do. After all, the Bible knows nothing of a static deity who remains aloof and uninvolved in the moving flux of nature and history. He is a very much involved God! He is a God who risks himself in his world in creative, reconciling, and renewing activity. He is a God of action, a God of history, a God of politics. Naming him and identifying his activity becomes, as Cox has said, "a question of where, in the push and pull of human conflict, those currents can be detected which continue the liberating activity we witness in the Exodus and in Easter." [28] It shall be our purpose in the next chapter to attempt to identify those characteristic activities in which his presence becomes manifest and his power becomes operative in the world.

[28] *The Secular City,* p. 242.

III

WHAT IS GOD DOING
IN THE WORLD?

The intent of this chapter is, as Harvey Cox has phrased
it, "to speak in a secular fashion about God"; or, in the
words of Gerhard Ebeling, to engage in "worldly talk of
God." The main thrust of our task and its practical implications for Christian mission is well summarized in
a statement by Albert H. van den Heuvel:

The discovery that the church is not the only tool God can or
does use to work in his world but is rather the announcer and
celebrator of his work, has not yet been fully digested, but has
attracted the attention of many, especially younger theologians.
It has made them scouts for the footprints of the Master in the
world, who conceive their primary task as discerning where
signs of God's presence in the world can be seen, so that they
may indeed celebrate them, point them out, and try to be faithful
to them.[1]

The hazards of such an undertaking, as I intimated in
the previous chapter, are obvious. To say "Lo, here" or
"Lo, there," and confidently to identify "where in the
world" God is to be found, and "what in the world" he is
doing, can lead us to a new domestication of God in the
trappings of our favorite ideology. Karl Barth's repeated
warnings on this score must be heeded. It is perilously
easy for Christians to confuse the "work of God" with
movements which comport with their own self-interest,
the interest of their group, or the interest of their nation.
It was this kind of idolatry into which the German Chris-

---

[1] Quoted in Colin Williams, *Faith in a Secular Age* (New York:
Harper & Row, 1966), p. 93.

tians fell during the Nazi era, a fact which explains Barth's strong emphasis upon the "otherness" of God and his hesitancy to identify, with any positive assurance, what God is doing in the world.

Despite the dangers involved, however, to abandon the attempt to read the signs of the times in the light of what God is doing in the world is to evacuate our talk about God of concrete content and meaning, and surrender it to transcendental irrelevance. Lacking concrete point and relevance, our speaking about God "provokes no opposition, yet neither is it heeded in revolutionizing ways, but spreads abroad that possibly tranquilizing, but actually killing, atmosphere of unimportance and boredom which is the death of faith." [2] Our speaking of God today must somehow bite into concrete, secular reality and provide leverage for real change in the world, if it is to be credible to many people.

In an age of science and technology in which, as Bonhoeffer has said, man has "come of age," it is easy for man to draw the conclusion that the only effective "powers" operative in the world are those which he himself has generated. One is reminded of the remark of William Hamilton's son as he and his father looked up at the stars and attempted to identify the heavenly bodies for a school assignment in astronomy: "Which are the ones we put up there, Dad?" In a technological age in which nature has been "disenchanted" and history "desacralized," theology has the prodigious task of showing that there is an extra-human power at work in the world which is affecting significantly the shape of events. Indeed, it is a life-and-death question for Christian faith today, as Karl Rahner has stated, "whether the Church can so faithfully testify to the

[2] Ebeling, *Word and Faith*, p. 360.

redeeming and fulfilling presence of that ineffable mystery whom we call God that the men of the age of technology, who have already made so many advances toward control of their world and destiny, can experience the power of this unspeakable mystery in their lives." [3]

To speak of God as a contemporaneous power of change in the world is to accent what traditional theology talked about under the doctrine of the Holy Spirit. God as Holy Spirit is God as *present reality* and *active power*. The Spirit, like the wind, has *the power to move things* mysteriously and unpredictably. "The wind blows where it wills and you hear the sound of it, but you do not know whence it comes nor whither it goes; so it is with every one who is born of the Spirit." (John 3:8) God the Holy Spirit does not restrict his operations, as some Christians have erroneously believed, to moments of ecstatic experience in which men "feel the presence of God." He may do his work in the world through those who are quite unconscious of his presence, who may, in fact, deny his reality, as was the case with the Persian emperor, Cyrus (Isa. 45). Today, he may accomplish his purposes through anyone from hippies to humanists, from Communists to Christians, who, consciously or unconsciously, serve as instruments of his judgment and his love.

In this chapter we shall focus on three basic ways in which the reality of God is present in the world as an active power. He is present and active: 1) as the power of creation, 2) as the power of humanizing change, and 3) as the power of a renewed and redeemed future. Hopefully, our analysis will afford us some concrete clues as to what it is that God is doing in the world and how, in turn, we may become participants in his ongoing work.

[3] *The Church After the Council* (New York: Herder and Herder, 1966), p. 26.

God as the Power of Creation

In the very first article of the creed, Christians confess their faith in the God of creation: "I believe in God the Father Almighty, maker of heaven and earth." In this simple but stupendous affirmation of faith, there is a wealth of meaning capable of illuminating our understanding of God, the world, and our place in it. Unfortunately, in the way in which it has often been presented, it has been reduced to an incredible pseudo-scientific assertion about the physical origin of the planet earth or the solar system. Langdon Gilkey's description of what the biblical idea of creation probably meant to the Christian of the eighteenth or nineteenth century reflects the naiveté with which some people still view the matter:

Not so very long ago (4004 B.C., in fact), God, having dwelt in splendid isolation for eternity, suddenly created in one series of momentous, instantaneous acts the whole present world. In this single miraculous series of events, centering somewhere in Mesopotamia, the Lord made in their present form all the kinds and species of things that were ever to be: the sun, the moon, and stars were given their places, our present seas, mountains, and valleys were formed by his direct power, the present species of plants and animals were made by His hand. Thus the whole world as we know it came to be, not by an age-long process of gradual development, but by the fiat of a fabulous artificer in six days of furious activity.[4]

If the space-age Joneses can't swallow that, what are we to put in its place as a credible, yet Christian, representation of God's creative work? Let us do what we can to unpack some of the meaning in the Christian doctrine of creation.

[4] *Maker of Heaven and Earth* (Garden City, N. Y.: Doubleday & Co., 1965), p. 18.

In the first place, it means that *the world is not self-sufficient or self-explanatory*. It means that, as a whole and in all of its parts, it is completely dependent upon a creative power which has brought it into being and continues to sustain it through every moment of its existence. To believe in God as Creator is to believe that, without his continuing creative and sustaining power, the world would collapse into the nothingness from which it has come. "The renewal of each creature in each succeeding moment of its existence," writes Gilkey, "is a victory of being over the non-being of temporal passage. In the onrush of temporal passage, this victorious recreation in the next moment is accomplished by a power beyond ourselves, since each creature is caught within the present and cannot establish itself beyond the present. Thus, without the continuing power of God each creature would lapse back into the non-being whence it came." [5]

It is doubtful that even modern secular man, in his much celebrated autonomy, is totally devoid of this sense of finite dependence upon an ultimate "ground and power of being." [6] His efforts to establish his self-sufficiency and security are much too compulsive to be able to conceal an underlying ontological anxiety which he feels in the face of his finitude. Theologians like Reinhold Niebuhr have always insisted that this kind of basic anxiety is not only not pathological, nor a sign of immaturity, but an essential mark of man's humanness, the source alike of his destruc-

[5] *Ibid.*, p. 95.

[6] Eschatological theology's preference for "the power of the future" over Tillich's "ground of being" as an ontological symbol for God has the advantage of avoiding a static notion of God which sanctifies the status quo. It runs the risk, however, of suggesting that God's creative and providential activity is restricted so exclusively to the future that past and present are bereft of any significant traces of the divine working. Both symbols can be useful, and mutually corrective, in illuminating the full scope of God's creative involvement in the world.

tiveness and his creativity. Some recent secular theologians, more impressed by man's power than his limits,
have been prone to overlook this fact. We would agree
with Thomas W. Ogletree in affirming that "if the Christian message is to speak to contemporary man, it must
learn to address him at the point of his strength, enabling
him to exercise his power constructively and redemptively." [7] But it must also continue to speak to him, as
Ogletree clearly recognizes, at the point of his limits, his
finiteness, his creaturely dependence. However spectacu-
larly man through his technological triumphs expands his
power and control over nature, however far out he moves
among the stars as a denizen of interstellar space, he
still must face the fact that he is going to die. And this
means that he does not have the power of being in himself.
That man and the world are absolutely dependent upon
the creative power of God to give them being and to sustain them in being is the primary affirmation of the Christian doctrine of creation.

To believe in God as the power of creation is also to
believe that *the world is good*. This is to say that everything that is has been created by God for a purpose, and
hence is not to be despised as evil. In the first chapter of
Genesis, God is represented as looking at each product of
his handiwork and saying "behold it was good." Every
being which is the fruit of God's creative love has its own
intrinsic and inalienable worth. It has this worth by the
very fact that God has loved it into being.

The Christian who acknowledges God as Creator will
therefore find it easy to celebrate spontaneously and joy-
fully all those natural powers and gifts which he has received from the hand of his Creator. He is thereby delivered from shameful and negative attitudes toward such

[7] *New Theology No. 6*, p. 50.

things as his bodily functions and passions, his sexual roles, his racial characteristics, his critical powers of reason. The grudging, distrustful, and censorious estimate of these gifts of nature by the Puritan mind, its despising of the earthy and the natural, is really a denial of the goodness of creation and a libel against the Creator himself.

The Black Revolution has been helping us to rediscover this meaning of the doctrine of creation in a new context. The rediscovery of the beauty of blackness is, in reality, a celebration of the goodness of one of God's created gifts. James H. Cone has written illuminatingly on this point:

For God to love the black man means that God has made him somebody. The black man does not need to hate himself because he is not white, and he should feel no need to become like others. His blackness, which society despises, is a special creation of God himself. He has worth because God imparts value through loving. It means that God has bestowed on him a new image of himself, so that he can now become what he in fact is.[8]

The worth and dignity of the black man, like the worth and dignity of all of us, is not something which he must earn, but something with which he is endowed, simply by the fact that he *is,* as a creature of the divine love.

It would be a grave theological error to assume that creation is something that took place in a specifiable time period at the dawn of the world's history and is now over and done with. *Creation is not a once-for-all event, but an ongoing process.* It involves all three modes of time—past, present, and future. This threefold functioning of God's creativity is succinctly summarized by Tillich: "God *has* created the world, he *is* creative in the present moment, and he *will* creatively fulfil his *telos.* Therefore, we must

[8] *Black Theology and Black Power,* p. 52.

speak of originating creation, sustaining creation, and directing creation." [9]

God, as the power of creation, is still dynamically at work in the world, bringing into being new worlds of order, beauty, and human community. Part of this continuing creative process has been delegated to *man as co-creator with God*. In the Genesis creation stories we read that man was placed in the garden "to till and to keep it" (Gen. 2:15). He was called to "subdue" the earth "and have dominion over the fish of the sea and over the birds of the air and over every living thing" (Gen. 1:28). In other words, man was given the freedom and the creative powers to begin to steer and to shape history. We are called to be trustees of creation, "laborers together with God" (I Cor. 3:9) in the building of his world.

Man's tremendous technological achievements, culminating in our time in his opening of a pathway to the moon, is but one expression of the way in which he shares in the ongoing creative purposes of God. Through imaginative social planning, through the search for more effective political institutions, through artistic and cultural productions—in all these ways, man continues the creative work of God in fashioning a more human world. Much more urgent and formidable challenges to his creative genius than more space trips to the moon or to Mars still lie ahead of him, namely, the building of those social structures and institutions which will make the cities of the earth fit habitations for human beings to live in.

In giving over to man this independent creativity, God has run the risk of having his creative purposes for his world thwarted and frustrated. Here we see clearly that *the very essence of the creative act is love*. "God is love," says the writer of I John. It is of the nature of love to free

[9] *Systematic Theology* I (Chicago: University of Chicago Press, 1951), p. 253.

the "other," to grant to the "other" an independent being over against us. This is what happens in creation. God does not, as it were, hoard up his being in himself. In creation he lets us go out from himself in independence and freedom. God's creative love is thus expressed in what John Macquarrie has described as a dynamic activity of "letting-be." [10] Creation, on these terms, inevitably means risk. Like the father in the parable of the prodigal son, God was willing to let man "go on his own" even at the risk that he would waste his substance in self-destructive living. He was willing to grant to men the "dread gift of freedom," even at the risk that that freedom might be abused in such a way that the very purposes of his creation would be subverted and endangered. This risk he was prepared to run in order that men might be brought to the maturity of true sons of God within a community of freedom and of love.

God as the Power of Humanizing Change

It might appear, from a cursory examination of the actual world in which we find ourselves, that God's monumental gamble in creation has scarcely paid off. An ugly rent has appeared across the fabric of God's created order introduced by the crown of his creation, *homo sapiens.* What God saw as "very good" man has succeeded in perverting and distorting into all manner of evil. War, racial conflict, poverty, polluted streams, poisoned air, crime, sexual perversion, family and personal disintegration—all these are eloquent testimony to the way in which man has botched up the world which God has made. Created to be free, his will to power has reduced him to bondage. Sum-

[10] *Principles of Christian Theology* (New York: Charles Scribner's Sons, 1966), p. 208.

moned into being by and for love, he has refused responsibility for his fellows and resisted the interdependence of community, within which alone the secret of his humanity is disclosed. Entrusted with the responsibility of being nature's caretaker, his lust for profit and convenience has caused him to violate her with rapacious destructiveness. Put into a world which was meant to be the theater of his growth into "mature manhood," he has managed to replace that world with one of his own making, a dehumanized and dehumanizing world of enslavement and alienation.

In a day when Dachau and Hiroshima are still vividly alive in our memory, when our cities are exploding with racial hostility and violence, when our world teeters crazily at the brink of nuclear confrontation, when the pollution of our environment and the man-made disruption of its ecological balance threatens our extinction, it would be easy to draw the pessimistic conclusion that God's experiment with the human race is doomed to failure. It is the audacious claim of Christian faith, however, that God is still alive and at work in our tragically disordered world, decisively engaging the destructive forces unleashed by men. He can be experienced in the midst of life as the power of liberation, reconciliation, and redemptive change.

Faith affirms that, in the midst of the dehumanizing forces which hold men in personal and social bondage, there is a countervailing power at work in the world. This power is referred to in the Bible as the "power of God for salvation" (Rom. 1:16), a power which brings wholeness and healing into man's individual and corporate existence. It is the power of a "new creation," a "new being" (Tillich), which is actively transforming an old corrupt, distorted world into a new one. In Paul's view, this power of transformation and renewal has entered into the historical process decisively and uniquely in Jesus Christ, and through him been released into the whole creation. "Therefore, if any man be in Christ, he is a new creation; the old has passed away, behold, the new has come." (II Cor. 5:17) The God who is manifested in Jesus Christ is the God who makes "all things new" (Rev. 21:5).

It is common in today's theology to identify the redemptive activity of God with those events and processes which are freeing men and society to become authentically human. Thus, J. C. Hoekendijk can refer to God as "that incorrigible Humanist." [11] And Paul Lehmann can affirm that "God has always been and is contemporaneously doing what it takes to make and to keep life human." [12]

According to this perspective, God is the source and power of all humanizing change in history. He is in the business of bringing men "to mature manhood, to the measure of the stature of the fulness of Christ" (Eph. 4:13). His "operative (real) presence and power" is at work in the world building up a "laboratory of maturity" in which man acquires "the power to be what man has been created and purposed to be." The maturity which is the goal of all God's creative and redemptive working is "the full development in a human being of the power to be truly and fully himself in being related to others who also have the power to be truly and fully themselves." [13]

In the Bible, God's humanizing work in the world is represented as taking place in a variety of characteristic activities which he pursues in relation to the evil forces and perverted structures of man's existence. We shall con-

[11] *The Church Inside Out* (Philadelphia: Westminster Press, 1966), p. 189.

[12] *Ethics in a Christian Context* (New York: Harper & Row, 1963), p. 101.

[13] *Ibid.*

centrate in the discussion which follows on three fundamental modes of his humanizing action.

God's Reconciling Action

The first element in God's humanizing mission in the
world is identified by the familiar theological concept of
reconciliation. In the passage in 2 Corinthians alluded to
earlier, Paul explicitly links God's ministry of reconciliation with the bringing into being of the "new creation" in
Christ. "All this is from God," he writes, "who through
Christ reconciled us to himself and gave us the ministry
of reconciliation; that is, God was in Christ reconciling
the world to himself" (II Cor. 5:18, 19). It is also clear
from New Testament teaching that reconciliation with
God is inseparable from reconciliation with ourselves and
with others. As Paul writes elsewhere, "He is our peace,
who has made us both one, and has broken down the dividing wall of hostility . . . that he might create in himself one
new man in place of the two, so making peace" (Eph.
2:14, 15).

Psychologists remind us that those who project hostility
and animosity toward their neighbors are likely to be
harboring a large reservoir of hatred and resentment toward themselves. Theologically, this self-hatred and inability to accept ourselves must be seen as rooted in an
even deeper alienation—our estrangement from the very
ground of our existence, God. Our rejection of ourselves and our rejection of others is usually bound up
with a pervasive sense of grievance and guilt in relation
to whatever it is that determines our life and destiny. Thus,
when we feel that "life" or "God" or "the universe" is
against us, we begin to depreciate ourselves and lash out
against others.

A vivid example of this cycle of alienation from self,

others, and God occurred in a recent encounter group. The group had been creatively, though painfully, grappling with the realities of the black revolution and its challenge to the Christian conscience. Midway through the week one woman, who had found the agony of confrontation too much to bear, broke out in bitter words of resentment over the fact that God had been mentioned so infrequently and so little time had been spent in prayer. When the leader thereupon called the group to prayer, she collapsed into tears. As she later poured out her honest feelings, it was quite clear that her sense of estrangement from God was all bound up with her sense of injury at being rebuffed by militant blacks and the confused and uncertain self-image which resulted. Here in microcosm was mirrored the tragic drama of estrangement, the scenario of which unfolds every day with such destructive consequences on the wider stage of history.

The power of God's reconciling action operates to arrest and reverse this disintegrative process. In its place there is initiated a process of healing which neutralizes the currents of hostility which flow between man and God and the neighbor. As Tillich has described it, healing in this context means "reuniting that which is estranged, gving a center to what is split, overcoming the split between God and man, man and his world, man and himself." [14]

This healing, reconciling action of God is proceeding in the world, sometimes on the initiative of the church's witness and mission, frequently without the benefit of an explicit religious label or sanction. Experience in the civil rights and peace movements of our day has convinced many Christians that God's work of reconciliation and humanization often goes on "incognito" among those who make no conscious profession of religious faith. This

[14] *Systematic Theology* II, 166.

should come as no surprise. The credibility of our Christian faith surely must find support in the assumption that there is a real power at work in the world—a reconciling, renewing, recreating power—a power which God does not jealously hoard up in ecclesiastical enclaves, but unleashes into all the world—a power which continues its healing, transforming work even when its source is not always acknowledged and celebrated.

The temptation to restrict God's work of redemption to what goes on in and through the church has its roots in the disastrous error of trying to keep redemption and creation in separate theological compartments. The New Testament knows no such separation. There Christ is represented as the agent not only of redemption, but of creation as well. "All things were made by Him; and without Him was not anything made that was made." (John 1:3) This means that God's purposes in redemption are continuous with his purposes for the whole of creation, *i.e.* "to gather together in one all things in Christ" (Eph. 1:10). What this implies for the cosmic and secular scope of God's redeeming action has been stated by Franklin H. Littell:

The map on which action takes place is universal, indeed cosmological. Christianity is not a precious cult of pigmy truths known only to the illuminated, and applying only to a fragment of creation. Christianity claims the Saviour to be Creator as well, the law of love to be the law of life. To claim that the redemptive process is limited to the Church is, from a Christian point of view, heretical. The Logos of God, the "hidden Christ," is working in secret ways to the redemption of the world. And there are many sons and daughters of the stranger, many who know not His name but bear the fruits of justice and righteousness, mercy and peace, who are being used of Him.[15]

[15] *The Church and the Body Politic* (New York: Seabury Press, 1969), p. 111.

If this is indeed true, we must be prepared to affirm that, wherever the "dividing walls of hostility" are being broken down between individuals, classes, races, and nations, God the Great Humanizer of History is at work. In one of his more memorable sermons, Tillich made the point this way: "Where one is grasped by a human face as human, although one has to overcome personal distaste, or racial strangeness, or national conflicts, or the differences of sex, of age, of beauty, of strength, of knowledge, and all the other innumerable causes of separation—there New Creation happens! Mankind lives because this happens again and again." [16]

Many of our modern cities are rapidly dying as viable human communities for the lack of such an effective power of healing reconciliation. The "walls of hostility" are being built ever higher—the suburbs against the inner city, the haves against the have-nots, white against black, the police against the ghetto, the bureaucratic elite against the restive masses, the blue-collar workers against the intellectuals, one political power block against another. And so the process of fracturing and fragmentation goes on, inexorably sapping the city of its wholeness and health. It is not too much to say that the very survival of the cities depends upon the generation of forces of social healing through finding some means of plugging into the power of God's reconciling action.

It is the momentous claim of Christianity that, through the power of reconciling love, God is building up out of the brokenness of human life, in however fragmentary and fragile a way, something that can be called authentic community. It believes in the ultimate sovereignty of divine love. Resourceful, tenacious, indiscourageable— that love is bringing about "the healing of the nations," the

[16] *The New Being* (New York: Charles Scribner's Sons, 1955), p. 23.

renewal of humanity, a transfigured creation. "For behold, I create new heavens and a new earth." (Isa. 65:17)

God's Judging Action

Much Christian discussion of reconciliation is hopelessly sentimental because it overlooks the cost in suffering to both God and man which genuine reconciliation entails. Too often it is represented as a painless patching up of differences on a "let's let bygones be bygones" basis. Christians who stand under the "sign of the cross" should know that reconciliation cannot be purchased that cheaply. It is a distorted and impoverished understanding of God's reconciling action which does not see it as inseparably linked with God's judging action.

Some nineteenth-century liberal theologians, such as Albrecht Ritschl, thought they were rendering the Christian faith more plausible by eliminating the idea of divine judgment and wrath as an outmoded anthropomorphism. Actually they were undermining the very credibility of the notion of divine love by reducing it, in effect, to a grandfatherly indulgence. Martin Luther saw more clearly into the essence of the Christian understanding of God when he pictured judgment and wrath as the "strange work" of love.

It was a recurring theme of the Old Testament prophets that God was active in judging Israel and the surrounding nations through the crises and catastrophes which befell them. In a typical statement Jeremiah represents God as declaring:

> The Lord will roar from on high,
>   and from his holy habitation utter his voice. . . .
> The clamor will resound to the ends of the earth,
>   for the Lord has an indictment against the nations;

he is entering into judgment with all flesh,
and the wicked he will put to the sword.
(Jer. 25:30, 31)

In the New Testament, the apostle Paul sees the wrath of God as expressing itself in the hardening of men's hearts and the dulling of their moral sensitivity to the point where they gradually become dehumanized. "The wrath of God," he writes, "is revealed from heaven against all ungodliness and wickedness of men who by their wickedness suppress the truth" (Rom. 1:18). This wrath expresses itself by allowing the lusts and idolatries of men to run their natural course into all sorts of moral perversions and intellectual self-deceptions.

If the biblical references to the judgment and wrath of God are to achieve credibility in the minds of men and women today, they will, of course, have to be divested of those anthropomorphic features which frequently picture a God of arbitrary vengeance and all-too-human petulance. So reinterpreted, the judgment of God can be a meaningful concept illuminating our present history and experience. An excellent statement of its meaning was included in a pastoral letter issued in 1958 by the Episcopal Bishops:

It is not some extraneous power falling upon us with no relationship to our behavior. It is not the capricious will of an arbitrary tyrant. . . . God's judgment is . . . the inevitable result we bring upon ourselves when we move against the grain of His universe. . . . It is God frustrating our purposes when we oppose His will. . . . You will find the judgments of God reported in your daily newspaper, in the clash and contradiction of rival ambitions and fears, in the hatred and suspicion we earn when we fail to deal justly with those with whom we share this narrow world.[17]

[17] Journal of the 1958 General Convention of the Episcopal Church, pp. 49-50.

Tillich implies much the same thing when he speaks of the wrath of God as "the emotional symbol for the work of love which rejects and leaves to self-destruction what resists it." [18]

We do not need to look far in our world today for concrete illustrations of God's judging action. We can see it clearly in the bitter, dehumanizing fruits of racial prejudice and segregation which are today convulsing our nation. The judgment of God on our corrupt and violent white civilization has ripened in recent years into a full-blown black revolution. One has only to read the hot, searing words of the literature of that revolution, books like Cleaver's *Soul on Ice* and *The Autobiography of Malcolm X,* to realize that, as we have sown the wind in race relations in our country, we must be prepared to reap the whirlwind.

The disorientation and confusion of white liberals in the present crisis stem, in large part, from their inability to come to terms with the reality of God's judging action as expressed in the turbulent events of recent times. Somehow they still cling to the sentimental illusion that reconciliation between the races can be effected by a little more love, a few more moral preachments about brotherhood, an acceleration of good will visits between blacks and whites. An angry young black theologian, James H. Cone, indicates what the response of black people must be to such sentimentalists: "We must inform them as calmly and clearly as possible that black people cannot talk about the possibilities of reconciliation until full emancipation has become a reality for *all* black people. We cannot talk about living together as brothers (the 'black and white together' attitude) as long as they do everything they can to destroy us." [19]

[18] *Systematic Theology* I, 284.
[19] *Black Theology and Black Power,* p. 146.

If Christians believe that a power of divine judgment is working itself out in the violent conflicts of the racial struggle, they cannot avoid the conclusion that that judgment must begin with the house of God. The Black Manifesto, with its demands for reparations from white churches for past injustices perpetrated against black Americans, must be seen in this light. Semantic disagreement over the appropriateness of the term "reparations," or alarm over the revolutionary rhetoric with which it was delivered, should not blind our eyes to the fact that here is a contemporary vehicle of God's judgment, calling the church to the most radical kind of repentance, restitution, and renewal.

Those who are unable to hear resounding through the angry and desperate voices of today's revolutionaries the voice of God's judgment against a corrupt and repressive society, are out of touch with the realism of the biblical prophets. They need to read again Amos and Hosea, Isaiah and Jeremiah. Those who think that the grave ills which beset our nation can be healed without abrasive confrontation and conflict, without disruption, violence, and suffering, are asking for a counterfeit which has no basis in biblical faith—reconciliation without a cross, love without justice. They need to remember that Jesus was crucified, not for being a harmless Galilean preacher, but for being a dangerous revolutionary who had the audacity to take on the cynical and corrupt power establishments of his day, both religious and political. They crucified him because he insisted on being a disturber of the peace.

What we have been saying about the "strange work" of God's love presupposes a dynamic understanding of the divine judgment as a real power of justice operative in the world, "a power that makes for righteousness." The biblical writers, in contrast to the Greeks, did not talk about justice as an abstract attribute of deity which provides some kind of eternal model to be contemplated and emulated in human patterns of justice. They saw God, rather, as actively involved in the messy rough and tumble of social and political struggle, "doing justice," and calling on men to "do justice" (Amos 5:24; Mic. 6:8; Jer. 22:15, 16).

The God of the prophets and of Jesus was no Olympian deity dispensing justice from on high in neutral and detached impartiality. In some ways his judgments were very partial. He took sides with the poor against the rich. He championed the weak against the powerful. His righteousness was characteristically expressed in his vindication of the needy and the fatherless, the exploited and the oppressed. It is precisely because of their defenselessness, Barth writes, that "God always takes his stand unconditionally and passionately on this side alone: against the lofty and on behalf of the lowly; against those who already enjoy right and privilege and on behalf of those who are denied it and deprived of it." [20]

If the vindication of the poor and the defense of the powerless is, indeed, part of God's humanizing mission in the world, then those of us who would share in that mission must resist the notion that we can assume a stance of moral neutrality in the struggles for social justice going on in our world today. It is a spurious understanding of reconciliation which suggests that the Christian ought to stand outside the conflict and be a kind of broker or mediator between opposing forces, without himself taking sides. Moltmann correctly identifies this posture as "the old ecclesiastical triumphalism in modern dress." In its attempt to view all worldly conflicts *sub specie aeternitatis*, it is a premature anticipation of the Kingdom of God. "Only through the dialectic of taking sides," he concludes,

[20] *Church Dogmatics* I/1, 386.

"can the universalism of salvation make its entrance into the world." [21]

To be sure, a Christian ministry of reconciliation in the midst of social conflict will seek to heal the differences between opposing groups in the power struggle and prevent excesses in self-righteous fury, hatred, and violence. At the same time, it will remember that to "do justice," in the biblical sense, is to be a partisan for the poor and the powerless. To participate in God's humanizing mission is to do battle with those great disparities of wealth and power which destroy human community by reinforcing the pride of the powerful and the resentments of the dispossessed. It is to be in the vanguard of those movements which marshal power in the interest of the weak and the exploited. It is to engage in the kind of social and political action which works for fundamental changes in dehumanizing structures and enslaving systems. Here is where the action is—God's judging and reconciling action to bring about humanizing change in the world.

God's Liberating Action

Implicit in all we have said is a third form of God's work of humanization—his liberating action. The ultimate goal of reconciliation and judgment is freedom—the freedom of man to become what he was created to be, truly and fully human. Freedom is an indispensable condition for being authentically human. "For freedom Christ has set us free." (Gal. 5:1)

The determined bid of the Negro for "black power" is not simply a demand for a bigger slice of social and economic justice. It is the unsuppressible striving for a

[21] *Religion, Revolution and the Future* (New York: Charles Scribner's Sons, 1969), pp. 140-43.

kind of human maturity and responsibility which can come only when one has the freedom to share in the shaping of one's own destiny. To be powerless, to have your existence defined for you by other people, to be the pawn of impersonal systems and forces which take away your power of self-determination—all this is to be dehumanized. If this be the case, Christians must interpret the "freedom movement" as a movement in which the power of God is at work to strike off the manacles which enslave men and keep them from their full humanity. "Black rebellion is a manifestation of God himself actively involved in the present-day affairs of men for the purpose of liberating a people." [22]

There are certain brands of pietistic and existentialist theology which are content to define freedom in a very circumscribed way as essentially an inward and spiritual liberty. The "liberty with which Christ has made us free" is pictured as an inner freedom which is independent of the external circumstances of our lives, and which is possible even when a man is in chains. While this kind of freedom is undoubtedly an essential part of the fruit of the Gospel, it by no means exhausts the scope of God's liberating action in human life. That action encompasses the "outer man" as well as the "inner man," social, economic, and political emancipation as well as spiritual freedom. It delivers men from the prison house of physical as well as spiritual poverty. It challenges all those "powers" which would tyrannize over men's bodies as well as their souls.

A religion which makes a man content with "soul liberty," while inspiring meek acquiescence in social conditions that stunt and enslave his total being, is worthy of the contemptuous Marxist epithet "an opiate of the people." Authentic Christian faith does not encourage men,

[22] James H. Cone, *Black Theology and Black Power*, p. 38.

black or white, red or brown, to accept the status of the "nigger," abdicating a large part of their humanity under the conformist demands of an oppressive society. It inspires, rather, the militancy of the freedom songs which call for "freedom now" from all the demeaning conditions of inhuman servitude.

Who can read through the Bible, from the Exodus to the Resurrection, and fail to note the same exhilarating celebration of revolutionary freedom? God is the great Deliverer who leads his people out of bondage. The children of Israel are made a nation by a divine act of deliverance from a real Pharaoh who had held them in economic and political servitude. When Jesus comes on the scene, he announces himself as the bearer of a messianic mission of emancipation from real slavery:

"The Spirit of the Lord is upon me,
because he has anointed me to preach the good news to the poor.
He has sent me to proclaim release to the captives
and recovering of sight to the blind,
to set at liberty those who are oppressed,
to proclaim the acceptable year of the Lord."

(Luke 4:18, 19)

If the church is to recover its lost credibility, it must begin to take seriously again that manifesto of God's liberating, humanizing mission. It must abjure the temptation to serve as a chaplaincy to the established order, with all its enslaving and dehumanizing tendencies, and join in God's revolution of freedom. "Christians should no longer confer on a repressive society the appearance of freedom, humanity and brotherhood through their political and social harmlessness. They can realize freedom only in intolerant opposition to the powers and spokesmen of the 'status quo,' while they demonstrate for the oppressed and become with the protesting the 'children of protest.' " [23]

God as the Power of the Future

We have been making bold, in the preceding sections, to trace the activities of God in the secular affairs of the world. We have sought to show the ways in which he is at work in the world as a creative and humanizing power for change. The upshot of our discussion has been something like this. To believe in the living God is to believe that he is somehow at work in the world where the significant action is—where men live and love, suffer and die, where their bodies are mangled by the machines of war and their spirits are beaten by chronic poverty, where they build cities and nations, political institutions and spaceships, where they hunger for bread, for freedom, for justice, and for love. Wherever in that world healing and reconciliation are taking place, wherever men struggle for human dignity, wherever they discover one another as brothers across walls of division and hatred, wherever sin and prejudice and injustice bear their bitter fruit and wherever love wins its victories—there faith sees God present and at work.

We were careful to point out in the beginning that all this is an affirmation of faith. The action of God in history is never so obvious or unparadoxical that it can be directly discerned. In a radically secularized world, says Johannes B. Metz, "no longer do we directly discover in the world 'traces of God,' but rather the 'traces of man' and his transforming activity." [24]

[23] Jürgen Moltmann, "Antwort auf die Kritik der Theologie der Hoffnung" in Wolf-Dieter Marsch, ed., *Diskussion über die "Theologie der Hoffnung"* (Munich: Chr. Kaiser Verlag, 1967), p. 235.
[24] "Creative Hope" in *New Theology No. 5* (1968), p. 132.

If this be so, are we not putting an intolerable strain on the credulity of the secular man of today by insisting that behind the transforming activity of man there lies a redemptive activity of God; that in and through the powers of nature and history there is expressed a creative, judging, and reconciling power of God? However wistfully he may want to believe, can he find such a faith credible? Here, of course, there can be no question of proof. In the final analysis, it may be *a question of hope*. "Until it gives us hope," says Miguel de Unamuno, "our faith is a formless faith, vague, chaotic, potential; it is but the possibility of believing, the longing to believe. But we must needs believe in something, and we believe in what we hope for." [25]

Contemporary man is much concerned about the future. He is increasingly aware that, with the tools of technology at his disposal, he has the capacity to create the kind of future he wants. At the same time, he is not unaware of the ambiguity which lurks in the possibilities of the future. The disastrous consequences of an unchecked population explosion or continuing environmental pollution, the tragedy of nuclear confrontation between the great powers, the growth of a "one-dimensional society" (Marcuse) in which man can lose his humanity in a homogenized social system—all these are real and not simply imaginary possibilities. For this reason, thoughtful men are increasingly cognizant of the profound perils of leaving the future to the mercy of accident or chance. The stakes are staggeringly high. Whether mankind can combine the moral and technical resources necessary for cashing in on the promise of a more human future, or whether it will bring the whole human experiment crashing down in a global

[25] *The Tragic Sense of Life* (London: Collins, The Fontana Library, 1962), p. 199.

catastrophe, is the haunting and unavoidable question which is forcing itself into the consciousness of men today.

In this context of concern for the future and the possibility of hope, the question of God is being raised anew today in a way which makes it compelling and inescapable even for modern secular man. It becomes the question of a power adequate to assure us of a renewed and redeemed future. It becomes the question of a viable ground for hope. The essential thrust of that question has been admirably expressed by Sam Keen:

The question of God is not the question of some remote infinite being. It is the question of the possibility of hope. The affirmation of faith in God is the acknowledgment that there is a deathless source of power and meaning that can be trusted to nurture and preserve all created good. To deny that there is a God is functionally equivalent to denying that there is a ground for hope. . . . If God is dead, then death is indeed God, and perhaps the best motto for human life is what Dante once wrote over the entrance to hell: "Abandon hope, all ye who enter." [26]

Some "death-of-God" theologians, notably William Hamilton, have attempted to delineate a Christian life-style characterized by love, but bereft of faith and hope. Such a life-style, however, bears less resemblance to the Christian perspective than it does to the life-stance of an Albert Camus who resolved to "think clearly and not hope any more" and to live life "without appeal" to any reality beyond the empirically observable facts of present experience.[27] Christian or not, the important question is whether such a humanism of love without hope can sustain itself amidst the negativities of existence that overwhelm the

[26] "Hope in a Posthuman Era" in *New Theology No. 5*, pp. 86-87.
[27] See *The Myth of Sisyphus* (New York: Vintage Books, 1960), pp. 3-48.

human spirit. Can love persist in its identification with human suffering and misery, can it bear the pain of being rebuffed and disappointed, unless it is upheld by some ultimate ground of hope?

In the final analysis, it is the God of hope, the God who is experienced as the power of a renewed and redeemed future, who gives us the freedom to love and the staying power to persist in that love. In Moltmann's words, "Hope makes us ready to bear the 'cross of the present.' It can hold to what is dead, and hope for the unexpected." [28]

This hope is a far cry from the cultural optimism celebrated by William Hamilton and predicated on the death of God. In his hymn to the new optimism written in 1966,[29] Hamilton appealed to the exuberance of the civil rights movement as evidence of the worldly optimism which is the fruit of the death of God. Is it fair to ask what has become of that optimism today? With the civil rights movement in a virtual shambles and the forces of reaction and repression on the ascendency, with Martin Luther King and Robert F. Kennedy in their graves, it may still be possible to sing "We shall overcome." But it is not self-evident that we can do so on the basis of any empirical prognostication of the future, on the assumption that God is dead. We *can* do so, I think, in the spirit of the parting words of Dr. King and sustained by the optimism of grace which he knew so well: "I have seen the promised land. I may not get there with you. But it doesn't matter now. We as a people will get to the promised land. My eyes have seen the glory of the coming of the Lord."

It is belief in "the coming of the Lord" which projects those horizons of hope which can alone undergird respon-

[28] *Theology of Hope,* p. 31.
[29] "The New Optimism—from Prufrock to Ringo" in *Radical Theology and the Death of God,* pp. 157-69.

sible Christian engagement in the revolutionary historical changes of our time. The God who did not die is the God of hope, the God who is the power of the future, the God whose coming kingdom of love and righteousness, peace and freedom, is constantly encroaching on every present. The paradox of his "hiddenness" in secular reality lies in the fact that the proof of his divinity still lies in the future. This means that, until "the kingdom of the world has become the kingdom of our Lord and of his Christ" (Rev. 11:15), and God has become "all in all," we are "saved by hope" (Rom. 8:24). In the perspective of hope, God is seen as both present and absent. *"God is present in the way in which his future takes control over the present in real anticipations and prefigurations. But God is not as yet present in the form of his eternal presence."* [30]

It is the future of God, his "not-yet-being," which is the dynamism of our future, the goad and the goal of our history. In the light of that hoped for future, we can make bold to identify and participate in those processes and events in our history which are a foretaste of his coming kingdom. Under the goad of that ultimate hope, we are driven into restless rebellion against those realities and structures of the status quo which impede and frustrate its fulfillment. According to Paul, this restlessness is shared by the creation itself. One can interpret his hymn of hope in Romans 8:18-24 as representing the conviction that a kind of cosmic striving is bringing the whole created universe to its ultimate fulfillment in the future of God. God as the power of the future is continually creating new possibilities of existence which expose the incompleteness and the bondage of the past and the present. The burden

[30] Moltmann, *Religion, Revolution and the Future,* p. 209.

of unfulfilled hope, however, is experienced as the birth-pangs of a coming liberation:

For I reckon that the sufferings we now endure bear no comparison with the splendour, as yet unrevealed, which is in store for us. For the created universe waits with eager expectation for God's sons to be revealed. It was made the victim of frustration, not by its own choice, but because of him who made it so; yet always there was hope, because the universe itself is to be freed from the shackles of mortality and enter upon the liberty and splendour of the children of God. Up to the present, we know, the whole created universe groans in all its parts as if in the pangs of childbirth. Not only so, but even we, to whom the Spirit is given as firstfruits of the harvest to come, are groaning inwardly while we wait for God to make us his sons and set our whole body free. For we have been saved, though only in hope.

(N.E.B.)

If we ask for the reason for this hope that is in us as Christians, we must turn to that event in history in which the kingdom of God is believed to have, in some sense, already come, and the future of God already been prefigured. That event is the person and mission of Jesus Christ, which is the final ground of Christian hope. What we are to make of this event today will be the concern of our next chapter.

PART THREE

CHRIST
OUR
CONTEMPORARY

IV

THE SEARCH
FOR AN AUTHENTIC CHRIST

At this point in our discussion we come to a particularly crucial stage in our search for Christian credibility. Christological considerations have always been pivotal in the work of theological construction. There are some, like Karl Barth, who go so far as to say that "there are strictly speaking no Christian themes independent of Christology." [1] However that may be, what we make of Jesus Christ is critically determinative of what we say about God and his work, man and his destiny, and the church and its mission. Christology is thus the linchpin of the whole structure of Christian belief. Where its truth-claims cease to be persuasive, the entire range of Christian theological affirmations begins to look questionable.

For centuries a great host of believers have found Christ to be the saving clue to the baffling enigmas of life and death. They have seen in him the author of their freedom, the anchor of their hope, and the pioneer of their salvation. Increasingly such exalted claims for a man who lived two thousand years ago strike men of our age as somewhat less than self-authenticating. They are prone to address to Jesus the words attributed to the madman of Gerasene: "What have you to do with me?" (Mark 5:7) On the lips of our contemporaries those words no longer carry any real animus against Jesus. They are more likely to express the blasé indifference of a generation which is simply not "turned on" by Jesus—at least the Jesus they have heard about in the churches. In the face of this lack of inner

[1] *Church Dogmatics*, II/1, 320.

THE SEARCH FOR CHRISTIAN CREDIBILITY

resonance for Jesus, Bonhoeffer's famous question from his prison letters becomes all the more urgent: "Who is Christ for us today?" It is perhaps not too much to say that the survival of the Christian faith as a credible option for modern man depends on the possibility of his finding a compelling and convincing answer to that question.

The Christ of Chalcedon

There seems little question that the way in which classical theology tried to understand the mystery of Christ makes little sense at all to us today. The orthodox understanding, hammered out as long ago as 451 at the Council of Chalcedon, depicted Christ as a God-Man who unites miraculously in his person two quite disparate natures or substances, one human and one divine. The framers of the Definition of Chalcedon used all the technical precision at their command to affirm that these two natures are distinct and yet indivisible elements in the one person of Jesus Christ:

Therefore, following the holy Fathers, we all with one accord teach men to acknowledge one and the same Son, our Lord Jesus Christ, at once complete in Godhead and complete in manhood, truly God and truly man, consisting also of a reasonable soul and body; of one substance with the Father as regards his Godhead, and at the same time of one substance with us as regards his manhood; like us in all respects, apart from sin; as regards his Godhead, begotten of the Father before the ages, but yet as regards his manhood begotten, for us men and for our salvation, of Mary the Virgin, the Godbearer; one and the same Christ, Son, Lord, Only-begotten, recognized in two natures, without confusion, without change, without division, without separation; the distinction of natures being in no way annulled by the union, but rather the characteristics of each nature being

96

preserved and coming together to form one person and subsistence.[2]

As a vehicle for communicating what Christ means for us today that kind of language and conceptuality is hopelessly inadequate and misleading. No doubt, in the day in which it was formulated, it served the church well as a protection against oversimplifications (heresies) which compromised the full reality of Christ as the definitive disclosure of both God and man. As for us, however, it neither speaks to us in terms which are intelligible, nor preserves the substance of an authentically Christian affirmation concerning Christ. As Bishop Robinson has reminded us, the way this formula for understanding Christ gets put together is a bit like mixing oil and water. "It is not surprising," he says, "that in popular Christianity the oil and water separated, and that one or the other came to the top." [3]

As a matter of fact, popular orthodox Christianity has always tended to stress the deity of Christ at the expense of his humanity. It has been more or less a replay of the ancient heresy of docetism.[4] This was a position which reduced the incarnation, in effect, to a charade in which God disguised himself temporarily in the garments of our humanity. In his superficial appearance Christ presented himself to men as a fellow human being. But this only *appeared* to be the case. Fundamentally he was a divine being—he was God.

Much orthodox piety today is similarly docetic. Here you

---

[2] Quoted from H. Bettenson, ed., *Documents of the Christian Church*, 2nd ed. (New York: Oxford University Press, 1963), p. 73.

[3] *Honest to God*, p. 65.

[4] Cf. W. Norman Pittenger's observation that "while docetism as a specific heresy has been condemned and is long since dead, there has been a persistent drive towards the docetic position which has often associated itself peculiarly with those who think of their view as rigidly orthodox." *The Word Incarnate* (New York: Harper & Brothers, 1959), p. 7.

have Christ pictured as a divine visitor from another world, who gets miraculously born into the human race through the supernatural process of a virgin birth, who accommodates himself for a brief span of time to the human condition, but who basically is not one of us. He is from out there. He represents an alien nature. His real nature is perceived not so much in the human dynamics of his psycho-physical existence as in those phenomena which transcend the human—his miraculous works, his supposed omniscience, his claims to divine status and authority.

Men and women of our day can be excused if they see in this characterization of Christ an unbelievable prodigy, an unreal phantom of the religious imagination, and an incredible claim on their emulation and loyalty. This de-humanized caricature actually bears little resemblance to the Christ of the gospels. However much the New Testament writers extol his uniqueness, they never lose sight of the fact that he was "made like his brethren in every respect." They see his authentic humanness as the essential pre-condition of his having any exemplary or saving relevance for us. "Because he himself has suffered and been tempted, he is able to help those who are tempted." (Heb. 2:18)

In whatever terms we describe the uniqueness of his relationship to God, we must not assume that it was the consequence of his having some kind of jump on the rest of us by virtue of his possession of some sort of super-natural character; that relationship was won as a real moral and spiritual achievement by dint of struggle, suffering, conflict, and faith. As impressed as we are by his penetrating insight into the secrets of the human heart, and his remarkable prevision of the course of human events, we dare not credit this to an extra-human power of omniscience; such powers of knowledge as he had did not exceed those of an acutely perceptive human mind, enhanced, to be sure, by an extraordinary spiritual sensitivity, but at the same time conditioned by the historically relative and limited knowledge-perspectives of his particular time and place.[5]

If Christ is to exercise any kind of irresistible attraction over the imagination of our contemporaries, we must find some alternative to the supernaturalistic model of understanding which makes it impossible for us to encounter him as an authentic human being. We must find ways of picturing him and interpreting him which do less violence, both to our present-day sensibilities and understandings, and to the way in which he actually encountered his own contemporaries. A credible Christ must be genuinely our contemporary as well as theirs.

Credibility and a Contemporaneous Christ

If the search for a contemporary Christ is to be our angle of approach, then we must take seriously Bonhoeffer's way of formulating the christological question: "Who is Christ for us today?" Bonhoeffer himself had no patience with investigations into what he called the "alchemy of the incarnation." He was convinced that, with respect to the incarnation, the question "How?" is both fruitless and presumptuous. Such questions as "how" Jesus was the revelation of God, or "how" a divine and human nature came together in Christ, are always illegitimate attempts on our part to deal with him on our own terms and compromise the integrity of his "otherness" by our own speculations. The only valid questions to address to Christ, Bonhoeffer insisted, were "Who?" or "Where?"[6]

---

[5] Cf. D. M. Baillie's excellent discussion of the various elements of Jesus' humanness. *God Was in Christ* (New York: Charles Scribner's Sons, 1948), pp. 11-20.

[6] *Christ the Center* (New York: Harper & Row, 1966), pp. 27-37.

While it may be debatable whether all "how?" questions must, or indeed can, be finally excluded from Christology, I find Bonhoeffer's choice of questions an excellent place to begin. It has the advantage of focusing our inquiry into the *mysterium Christi* on the personal rather than the metaphysical, on the concrete instead of the abstract. Theology today has the task of clearing away the jungle of metaphysical abstractions which have so long barred men's way to Christ and facilitating a fresh encounter with his sovereign person. It must find new ways of pointing out "who" he is for us today, and "where" he is to be found in the push and pull of contemporary events, if he is to "come alive" for us again with meaning and power.

But where are we to begin in our attempt to discover his person and his whereabouts? I would suggest that there is no better place to begin than where his first disciples began in the days of his flesh. We tend to forget that, for the original followers of Jesus, their faith in him as Savior or as Son of God did not emerge suddenly and full-blown as the consequence of any advance notice they had received of his supernatural status and powers. The stories about his virgin birth and pre-existence were only subsequently developed as ways of helping them to articulate a faith which they already had. Nor were they swept off their feet by any blinding theophany in which his deity was plainly announced. "Through what steps did the original disciples come to encounter God in and through Jesus? They first became acquainted with Jesus simply *as a man* to whom, for whatever reasons, they were attracted. Only *after* they knew him in this way and *on this presupposition* did they come to believe that in him God was present to them in some special way." [7]

The Gospels clearly portray a gradual process through

[7] Kaufman, *Systematic Theology: A Historicist Perspective,* p. 172.

which the disciples got to know Jesus at ever more intimate levels, until the realization finally dawned on them
that there was something in the form and quality of his
humanity which could not be explained adequately in
normal human categories. When Jesus finally posed the
question "Who?" in relation to his own person at Caesarea
Philippi, Peter was ready to venture the judgment that he
was the long-awaited Messiah of God. But this was a discernment of faith, the significance of which was only par-
tially and haltingly grasped at that time. It was not an
empirically demonstrable proposition. "Flesh and blood
has not revealed this to you, but my Father who is in
heaven." (Matt. 16:17) It is doubtful whether this growing awareness of the disciples concerning the uniqueness
of their Rabbi was at all clear cut and decisive until
after his death and resurrection.

This gradual process of faith-discernment by which the
disciples finally came to acknowledge the Lordship of
Christ has its corollary in a certain "divine incognito"
with which God was present to men in the human person
of Jesus. Jesus himself clearly rejected any attempt to
authenticate his divine mission by objective demonstrations of supernatural power. The thought of convincing
people by a public spectacle in which he would throw himself down from the pinnacle of the temple and be saved
by angelic intervention was turned aside as a temptation
of the devil (Luke 4:9-12). He characteristically opposed
the kind of mentality which is always looking for these
kinds of objective "signs" (Matt. 12:39).

The image of Jesus as a miracle-monger is a dangerous
and misleading one for two reasons. First, the very notion
of miracle as we understand it today (*i.e.* an event which
runs counter to natural law) is anachronistic when applied
to the accounts about Jesus. What the men of the Bible
identified as "miracle" was any event through which they

were grasped in a special way by the presence and activity of God. However extraordinary they might be, however much they might transcend what is usually considered "normal," these "wonders" were still natural events interpretable (from *our* perspective) as occurring in a cause and effect nexus. To be sure, the original events often underwent, over a period of time, a process of mythological transformation as a result of which they began to take on the appearance of magical signs. This process and its unfortunate effects is described by John Macquarrie as follows: "The inflation of the natural event into the spectacular sign is the way by which the mythological mentality seeks to express the distinctiveness and significance of the event for religious faith. But God's acting or his presence cannot be proved by publicly observable events, and the attempt to transform the miracle into a public prodigy ends up by obscuring and discrediting the genuine miracle, understood as revelatory event." [8]

This leads to the second reason why we must reject the notion that Christ authenticates himself and his mission by means of miracles as we commonly understand them today. Such a notion undercuts the correlation between revelation and faith. It does this by substituting the coercion of massive public evidence for the inner conversion and convincement of true faith. Faith in Christ on the basis of miracles is the mark of a superficial credulity; it does not grow out of the kind of genuine credibility which resonates with the deeper springs of our personal being, motivations, and commitments. Bonhoeffer says the same thing in somewhat more traditional language:

Had Christ proved himself by miracles, we would "believe" the visible theophany of the Godhead, but it would not be belief

[8] *Principles of Christian Theology,* p. 229.

in the *Christus pro me*. It would not be inner conversion, but acknowledgment. Belief in miracles is belief in a visible epiphany. Nothing happens in me if I assert my belief in miracles. There is only faith where a man so surrenders himself to the humiliated God-man as to stake his life on him even when this seems against all sense.[9]

In any authentic encounter with Christ, something *does* happen to us. In the concrete forms and features of his historical existence as a man we are constrained to see the definitive shapes of God's activity for us in the world, an activity which claims us and moves us to specific kinds of action and commitment of our own. It is not as if we already knew who God was, and have then simply to identify in Jesus the objective and demonstrable marks and attributes of deity. The so-called "deity of Christ" is not an objective fact for which evidence can be marshaled. To confess Jesus as the Christ is to stake our lives on the belief that in this man as nowhere else God is present and at work in a definitive way. To affirm the deity of Christ can mean nothing else than the acknowledgment that we have found in him the fundamental clue to the meaning of our lives and the destiny of our world. It is not to say "Jesus *is* God"; it is to confess that in Jesus we *see* God, the ultimate reality with which we have to do, uniquely focused in his human person and actions. For "he who has seen me, has seen the Father" (John 14:9).

This confession of faith, however, cannot be coerced by authoritative and arbitrary pronouncements of a "high Christology" which bludgeon people into assenting to extravagant claims of Jesus' divinity. If the church is to bring men and women in our day to a meeting with Jesus as the Christ, it must first simply invite them to look at Jesus from the vantage point of his original disciples. It

[9] *Christ the Center*, pp. 114-15.

must introduce them to Jesus the man. Unfortunately, its evangelistic efforts have usually started at the other end. It has proclaimed to them the "Christ of faith," the Christ elaborated theologically in the creeds, as the pre-condition of an accredited faith. As Bishop Robinson has so well put it, "they have not been called to work out the sum for themselves, to discover the authority *in* the experience, the revelation *in* the relationship, as the first disciples had to before, and again after, the Resurrection." [10] Particularly in a world "come of age," such an approach surely violates all canons of credibility.

A Christology from Below

What I am recommending as our method of exploration is what is called by theologians "a Christology from below." A Christology "from below" begins with the historical person, message, and actions of the man Jesus and finds in these the basis for recognizing whatever divinity he may possess. A Christology "from above," on the other hand, starts with his divinity and asks how the Son of God, the second person of the Trinity, becomes incarnate in the humanity of Jesus. The differences in these two approaches are not inconsiderable from the standpoint of our goal of Christian credibility. Wolfhart Pannenberg has faulted the second approach for three excellent reasons: 1) It arbitrarily presupposes the divinity of Jesus rather than showing how Jesus' actual history gives rise to such a belief. 2) It is so preoccupied with the problem of how God and man are united in the incarnation that it "recognizes only with difficulty the determinative significance inherent in the distinctive features of the real, historical man, Jesus of Nazareth," and 3)

[10] *The New Reformation?*, p. 37.

104

It ignores our "historically determined human situation," and asks us *per impossible* "to stand in the position of God himself in order to follow the way of God's Son into the world." [11] These are all persuasive reasons for rejecting the commonly employed approach of a Christology "from above," which makes the mistake (pointed out long ago by Ritschl) of "confessing the divinity of Christ before it is established in his works." [12]

I am aware that an approach to Christology which takes its orientation from the Jesus of history runs against powerful currents in recent theology, stemming largely from Barthian and Bultmannian sources. Neo-orthodox theologians have been inclined to follow Kierkegaard in his opinion that the only kind of contemporaneity with Christ which is possible or necessary is the contemporaneity of faith. For this reason, Jesus' own contemporaries had no advantage over those of us who came later, nor is it necessary for us to receive from them any testimony to the concrete impression which the historical figure of Jesus made on them. The *reductio ad absurdum* of this attempt to evacuate the Christ of faith of any significant historical content is found in this incredible assertion of Kierkegaard: "If the contemporary generation had left behind them nothing but the words, 'we have believed that

[11] *Jesus—God and Man* (Philadelphia: Westminster Press, 1968), pp. 34-35. Unfortunately, Pannenberg's own working out of a Christology "from below" is marred by a considerable failure to portray the concrete figure of the historical man Jesus. As a consequence his book, while making an impressive contribution to christological reflection, shows the same stultifying abstractness which has characterized too much traditional Christology. His problem may, at least in part, stem from the fact that he wishes to move from the "below" to the "above" too quickly, occupying himself with the historical Jesus only long enough to establish the necessity and factuality of the resurrection as the fulcrum of his dogmatic system. A Christology based so exclusively on the resurrection, however, is bound to be a highly artificial and forced abstraction from the concrete totality of the Christ-event.

[12] Quoted in *ibid.*, p. 208.

in such and such a year God appeared among us in the humble figure of a servant, that He lived and taught in our community, and finally died,' it would be more than enough." [13] While neo-orthodox writers generally would not want to go that far, they tend to endorse Kierkegaard's repudiation of the theological significance of the historical Jesus.

It is no wonder that a reaction to this kind of arbitrary fideism and its ruthless denigration of history has set in, in the form of a renewed "quest of the historical Jesus." The hazards in this undertaking are many, as was amply demonstrated by the original "quest" so devastatingly debunked by Albert Schweitzer. Disappointingly, most of the nineteenth and early twentieth century "lives of Jesus" revealed more about their authors and the times in which they lived than about Jesus himself. A famous remark by Father George Tyrrell illustrates well this danger of reading our own perspectives and prejudices into the story of Jesus: "The Christ that Harnack sees, looking back through nineteen centuries of Catholic darkness, is only the reflection of a Liberal Protestant face, seen at the bottom of a deep well." [14]

Let it be acknowledged that any attempt to get in touch with the concrete historical figure of Jesus entails a risk —the risk, namely, of confusing the reflection of our own cultural and theological face with the face of Jesus Christ. But it is a risk which must be run if Jesus is not to remain

[13] Quoted in D. M. Baillie, *God Was in Christ*, p. 49. Baillie's criticism of Kierkegaard on this point is worth repeating: "If the 'divine incognito' remains in this extreme form, what saving virtue is there in the dogma of the Incarnation? If there is no revelation, no 'unveiling,' of God in the human personality and career of Jesus, but only a 'veiling'; if God in Christ is as much as ever a *deus absconditus,* not a *deus revelatus;* what are we the better of the coming of God in Christ?"

[14] *Christianity at the Cross-Roads*, 2nd ed. (London: Allen and Unwin, 1963), p. 49.

"a dead fact stranded on the shores of time." It is of the utmost importance, however, *how* we proceed with the task of claiming him as our contemporary. I would like to suggest that authentic contemporaneity with Christ can be established only when we succeed in bringing together Christ *as he really was* and Christ *as he is for us today.* To try to get at either Christ without the other is to miss both.

The real Jesus of history is inevitably missed by purely objective methods of historical research. Scientific historical criticism, of course, is an indispensable tool in enabling us to sort out the documentary evidences of the historical Jesus. Certainly the account we give as to who Jesus was must be different today than it was before the advent of modern historical criticism. By themselves, however, historical-critical methods cannot tell us who Jesus really was. At best they provide us with a succession of photographs of some of the external features of Jesus' life and career, when what faith needs is something more like a portrait that tells us something about his significance for us. Jesus as he really was is accessible to us only when we begin to see in what he did and said and suffered something of the reality, meaning, and promise of our own lives today.

The Christ for us today is just as surely missed by purely existential methods of appropriation. To be sure, a large part of the christological task must be devoted to showing how the Christ-event illuminates the structures of our present existence and grounds our hopes for the future. It can do this successfully, however, only when its thinking is vitally controlled by the concrete picture of Jesus as he actually was in the days of his flesh. As Melanchthon said in the sixteenth century, we can know Christ only "through his benefits." But how he can benefit us today is not at all evident unless we are clear as to who the concrete figure in history is who offers these benefits to us.

This is one way of describing what theologians have referred to as the hermeneutical circle. We can know who Jesus really was only as we know who he is for us today; and conversely, we can grasp his significance for us today only when we are in turn grasped by the concrete reality with which he confronted his contemporaries. The language of the Trinity has been employed to express essentially the same insight in another way. Only as the Holy Spirit opens our eyes to the presence of the ultimate ground and truth of all reality (i.e. the Logos) in the man Jesus, can he be a contemporaneous power in our lives today.

The Quest for Concrete Images

Today the Christ of history has faded into the mists of unreality for vast numbers of people for the want of images vital and compelling enough to mediate his reality to their contemporary experience. Samuel H. Miller has rightly observed that "it is the image that keeps the connection between meaning and reality plain." "What we need," he says, are "ways by which we continually pour the concrete, living world back into the symbols and shapes of meaning, or by such constructions elicit old meanings from new circumstances in the world." [15] What we need in relation to our search for a truly contemporary Christ are images of relevance and elucidatory power which forge convincing connections between the real Jesus of history, the concrete situations in which he is to be encountered today, and the anticipated directions of his activity in the future. Our task is to locate and elaborate those germinal, liberating images of Christ which are

[15] *The Dilemma of Modern Belief*, p. 27.

capable of fusing together a symbolic synthesis of reality, meaning, and hope. They must be images which make it possible for the Christ of the past to light up our present and point the way to our future.

It should be made clear that when I recommend the use of images as a "way into" the mystery of Christ I am not talking about an arbitrary and fanciful exercise of the imagination which abandons the bedrock of historical reality. Christological images bear some resemblance to scientific models in the way in which they serve as essential media of disclosure of an ultimately mysterious reality which gives itself to us in no other way.[16] Needless to say, I am not using the notion of "image" in the sense in which we talk about a politician brushing up his image in preparation for an election campaign. Jesus does not need that kind of cosmetic assistance from us! He can do very well without the help of theological "make-up" artists. He *does* need, however, the kind of elementary gripping images which mediate to us fresh insight into his reality and abiding functions in the life of our world. The gospels are full of references to vivid images which he himself is reported to have used to communicate to his contemporaries the significance of his person and ministry—the images, for example, of shepherd, servant, Son of Man, Son of God, vine, door, the bread of life, the way, the light of the world.

Unfortunately, theology has not taken this precedent very seriously. It has been reluctant to commit the treasure of christological truth to the earthen vessels of concrete, contemporary imagery. As a consequence, John McIntyre's

[16] Cf. John McIntyre's chapter on "Models in Christology" in *The Shape of Christology* (London: SCM Press, 1966). Cf. also Frederick Ferré, "Mapping the Logic of Models in Science and Theology" in Dallas M. High, ed., *New Essays on Religious Language* (New York: Oxford University Press, 1969).

indictment is true: "Theology has been singularly slow to allow imagination a place within its sacred precincts; and one ought not to be surprised if as a result a good deal of theology has been correspondingly unimaginative." [17]

When it *has* allowed concrete images to play a role in its thinking, traditional theology has too often turned to archaic religious images which no longer embody the concerns nor stimulate the sensibilities of modern secular men. Dorothee Sölle has pointed out, that after a period in the eighteenth century in which "men were not afraid to find new names for Christ and to give fresh currency to old and already familiar ones," theologians reverted to older images like King, Lord, Shepherd and Redeemer, "pictorial terms to which historical distance lent enchantment and whose very lack of immediacy seemed to promise protection against criticism and decay." "At this time," she goes on, "when the real difficulties of translating the faith from a completely vanished age into our modern period were increasing, the theologian—like the priests in the Old Jerusalem temple—put back into circulation for special religious purposes a sacred coinage long since discarded. Current secular terms, which might have been used to denote Christ, had no business in the temple." [18]

The Secular Christ

If we are to image Christ in such a way as to make him credible to modern man, we must portray him as pre-eminently the secular Christ. Such a portrait is necessary, not only because this is the only Christ with which men today can identify, but because this is, in fact, the Christ pictured in the Gospels. The figure of Jesus has been

[17] *Ibid.*, p. 173.
[18] *Christ the Representative* (London: SCM Press, 1967), pp. 12-13.

painted over for so long by the sentimental gloss of religious piety that we may have difficulty in grasping this
elementary fact. A statement from John Oman, written
long before the recent surge of secular theologies, may
help to right our perspective:

In the life of Jesus nothing is more conspicuous than his meager
interest in specially sacred doings, and his profound interest in
the most ordinary doings of the secular life. In his parables the
only figures from the special religious life of a specially religious
time are the Pharisee praying with himself in the Temple and the
Priest and the Levite turning aside on the road to Jerusalem—
self-approving and little-approved men, solitary to their heart's
core. But what a varied secular procession of kings and slaves,
bailiffs and debtors, and farmers and fisherfolk, and housewives,
and children, and all at their secular occupations, with more
feasting than fasting, and more marriages than funerals.[19]

According to Bonhoeffer, it is a gross distortion of Christ
to portray him as either the prototype of the religious man
or as the object of religious devotion. "Christ is no longer
an object of religion, but something quite different, indeed and in truth the Lord of the world." [20] He does not
call us to a provincial otherworldly life of religious piety.
"He does not lead man in a religious flight from this world
to other worlds beyond; rather he gives him back to the
earth as its loyal son." [21] It is not on the sacred peripheries
of life that we meet Christ, but in the very lifestream of
the secular—"in the centre of the village." It is not through
some marginal religious faculty that he exercises his power

[19] *Grace and Personality* (London: Cambridge University Press, 1919),
pp. 75-76.

[20] *Prisoner for God*, p. 123.

[21] "Thy Kingdom Come" in John D. Godsey, *Preface to Bonhoeffer*
(Philadelphia: Fortress Press, 1965), p. 29.

over us. "Christ takes hold of a man in the center of his life." [22]

It was this essentially secular appeal to the people of his day, and the thoroughgoing secularity of his life-style, that more than anything else aggravated his relationships with the Scribes and Pharisees. They were infuriated by the cavalier way with which he treated their religious customs and conventions, notably those having to do with the Sabbath laws and fasting. "They looked for a religious Messiah coming to them from the world of the temple and the cult; but instead he came as a lay figure in the secular world—the Man who in his care for others revealed that he came to give man a truly human existence within the full context of the world of creation." [23]

For too long our imagination has kept Christ imprisoned in "the stained-glass jungle" of the church. The artists of Christendom have too frequently invited us to look at representations of Christ as a melancholy religious ascetic or an ethereal wraith of a man crowned with a halo of otherworldly transcendence. The truly revealing images of Christ in our time will, in their unrelenting secularity, break the bonds of his captivity to the sacred. They will put him back into the world where he belongs, the world for which he lived and suffered and died.

The secular image of Christ is, at the same time, an image of hope. It is an image which discloses the tendencies toward the future latent in the Christ-event itself. It is an image which has the power to release us from the confining restrictions of the present and summon us along the road to an open future. Imagination and hope are always natural allies. Imagination, says William F. Lynch, is "the gift that envisions what cannot yet be seen, the gift

[22] *Prisoner for God*, p. 154.
[23] Williams, *Faith in a Secular Age*, p. 51.

that constantly proposes to itself that the boundaries of the possible are wider than they seem." [24] An imagination brought into captivity to Christ will help us to break through the barriers of seeming impossibility and open up to us the future which has been pioneered by him.

An authentically secular image of Christ serves not only to kindle our hopes but to challenge us to revolutionary action. It commits us in concrete ways to a share in Christ's world-transforming mission. It draws us irresistibly into obedience to his vision of a new heaven and a new earth. When Saul Alinsky, the pioneer of the urban community organization movement, was asked why it was always church people who initiated and supported his organizations around the country, he gave this illuminating reply: "It is in the Judeo-Christian tradition that one finds the metaphors and images for transformation. This people has within its corporate memory the archetypal symbols which express and respond to revolutionary action for justice." [25] It shall be our task to identify some of these archetypal images from our tradition which have the power to energize us for Christ's humanizing, world-transforming mission.

A Symbolic Center

We are now ready to narrow our search for those images of Christ which hold the most promise for disclosing his authentic historical reality and his dynamic relevance for our mission today. There is, of course, a superabundance of christological images in the New Testament itself. For one reason or another, some of these are more capable

[24] *Images of Hope* (Signet Books; New York: New American Library, 1965), p. 27.
[25] Quoted in David O. Woodyard, *To Be Human Now* (Philadelphia: Westminster Press, 1969), p. 137.

than others of provoking an existential response in us today. This should not surprise us. It simply reflects the historical vicissitudes of all symbols and images: "What excites and satisfies one epoch is utterly lifeless to another; what arouses intense reaction in one age may not have power enough in another to cause a person to raise an eyebrow in passing. A metaphor may indeed be something like revelation, disclosing an unsuspected unity of relationship, or it may be a mere cliché, worn out by custom and no longer capable of surprise." [26]

Many of the New Testament images of Christ are incapable of gripping our imagination with any compelling immediacy, because they are so conditioned by the history of the time that they require the mediation of technical scholars to put us in touch with their meaning. For this reason, terms like Messiah or Son of God are no longer very serviceable to us. Other designations like King or Lord have the drawback of being associated in our imaginations with the panoply of a medieval court, and carry authoritarian and even totalitarian connotations which should have no place in our thinking about Christ. This is not to say that these terms and others like them ought to be completely ignored. But they can no longer provide the symbolic center for our interpretation of Jesus without dangerous distortion.

In the chapter which follows, I propose to construct such a symbolic center around three basic images of Christ as *the gracious neighbor, the joyous revolutionary,* and *the invincible pioneer.* It seems to me that these three images are more likely candidates than any others for doing the job of integrating the biblical testimony concerning Christ and providing an imaginative focus for appropriating his meaning for our secular age.

[26] Samuel H. Miller, "The Clown in Contemporary Art" in *Theology Today* (October, 1967), p. 318.

It might be objected that this is a rather arbitrary pro-
cedure which focuses on certain facets of the biblical picture of Christ while overlooking others. It is a method,
however, which has ample precedent in the gospels themselves. As Van A. Harvey has pointed out, the "memory-
images" which they record are similarly selective. Here
"we are presented with something like a bas-relief in
which everything unessential from the standpoint of the
sculptor has been chiseled away until nothing remains
but its basic pattern, or *Gestalt*." [27] Selectivity does not
necessarily mean, however, that the Christ-event has been
arbitrarily distorted and misrepresented. "A significant
pattern has been worked loose from the event, a pattern
that reflects, of course, the specific interest and perspective of the community. But the pattern is not an arbitrary
one . . . it is a creative and interpretive response to an
historical event." [28]

The three images we will be considering are selected
from the fund of memory-images left us by the original
witnesses. I have picked these three over others because
of their relatively greater promise for creating a *Gestalt*
capable of mediating the main outlines of the apostolic
testimony concerning Christ in terms that are meaningful
to us today. They are, in a sense, telescopic images which
recapitulate and gather up many other images and events
which make up the total story of Jesus' life and teaching,
death and resurrection.

These images of Christ are basically functional images.
They describe with a degree of concreteness what Jesus
actually did as it has significance for us. Not only do they
delineate different aspects of his mission in the world,
but they show how we are implicated in that mission.

[27] *The Historian and the Believer* (New York: The Macmillan Co.,
1966), p. 269.
[28] *Ibid.*, p. 258.

Too often the traditional titles ascribed to Christ have been largely honorific designations, which have held Christ up for personal adulation, but have done very little (at least for the contemporary imagination) by way of specifying for the Christian "the environment and direction of what he is to do." [29] Calvin's discussion of the threefold office of Christ as priest, prophet, and king was originally proposed as a step in this direction. As a matter of fact, a rough analogy may be discerned between these three traditional offices or functions of Christ and the images which we will be examining in the next chapter. Something of the priestly function is to be found in the image of the gracious neighbor, the prophetic function in the image of the joyous revolutionary, and the kingly function in the image of the invincible pioneer.

---

[29] Lehmann, *Ethics in a Christian Context,* p. 116.

V

IMAGES OF CHRIST
FOR A SECULAR AGE

Who is Christ for us today? We are powerless to give a credible answer to that question unless we are attuned to hear with sensitivity and compassion the agonized cries of a tortured world pressing in on us from every side. The world in which we seek to meet Christ as our contemporary is a world which still slaughters its innocents, stones its prophets, crucifies its saviors, and chains its slaves. It is a world in which "while fifty-five million people starve to death each year, the *Unpoor* squander astronomic sums on advertising to tickle the jaded appetites of their overstuffed people."[1] It is a world in which, in the name of free enterprise, giant corporations are allowed to keep migrant laborers in conditions of virtual peonage. It is a world in which flaming napalm defoliates forests and crops and incinerates untold thousands of innocent victims. It is a world in which millions of people are imprisoned in stinking, rat-infested slum ghettos with no chance of escape.

The Gracious Neighbor

In what guise is it possible for us to identify Christ in such a world as this? The first image, through which we may be able to identify him, has been suggested by Horst Symanowski, an industrial missioner in Germany:

[1] Colin Morris, *Unyoung—Uncolored—Unpoor* (Nashville: Abingdon Press, 1969), p. 79.

THE SEARCH FOR CHRISTIAN CREDIBILITY

The question of previous ages . . . "How can I find a gracious
God?"—this was the question that drove men, was the motor of
their behavior in the world, unleashed crusades and started wars.
It drove men and wouldn't let them sleep. But how many people
today are awakened to rise and seek an answer to this question?
Most of us sleep pretty well on it. Either we don't ask it, or it
appears to us as a mere historical, antiquated question. But
another question does drive us around, unsettles us, agitates
whole peoples, and forces us into anxiety and despair. "How
can I find a gracious neighbor?" How can we still live together?
Man and wife, superiors and subordinates, colleagues in com-
petitive struggle, and finally one people with another, East and
West?[2]

Who can doubt that the question about the "gracious
neighbor" is the cardinal question which men are asking
today in our conflict-ridden world? Anyone who has
participated in the civil rights movement has recognized
that question innumerable times—hardly ever expressed,
of course, in so many words—sometimes translated into
a torrent of angry resentment, sometimes finding the tones
of a quiet, desperate resignation. I remember being called
one midnight to the home of a black family which was
being harassed by a bigoted white neighbor who resented
their moving next door. The husband and father was away
fighting for "freedom" in the jungles of Vietnam. There is
still etched in my memory the terror-stricken face of the
mother as she waited for another rock to come hurtling
through the bedroom window of her eleven-year-old boy.
From that face came mutely but unmistakably the same
tormented question: "How can I find a gracious neighbor?"

Christ comes into our cities of alienation and fear today,
as he did in the days of his flesh, as none other than the

[2] *The Christian Witness in an Industrial Society* (Philadelphia: Westminster Press, 1964), p. 50.

gracious neighbor. He stands alongside all the "wretched of the earth" as their servant and as their fellow-sufferer. James H. Cone has it right when he says:

If the gospel is a gospel of liberation for the oppressed, then Jesus is where the oppressed are and continues his work of liberation there. Jesus is not safely confined in the first century. He is our contemporary, proclaiming release to the captives and rebelling against all who silently accept the structures of injustice. If he is not in the ghetto, if he is not where men are living at the brink of existence, but is, rather, in the easy life of the suburbs, then the gospel is a lie.[3]

One cannot read the gospel record without stumbling on the image of the gracious neighbor again and again. Here Christ is characteristically encountered in the role of the humble servant who gives himself radically to others in a ministry of self-emptying love. "The Son of Man came not to be served but to serve." (Matt. 20:28) "For which is the greater, one who sits at table, or one who serves? Is it not the one who sits at table? But I am among you as one who serves." (Luke 22:27) One of his best-loved stories, the Parable of the Good Samaritan, is the story of a gracious neighbor who risks his life to bind up the wounds of a fellow-human being in distress. In another great parable, Jesus' picture of the Last Judgment, he leaves no question in our mind as to those who are destined to win his approval in the final reckoning. They are unmistakably the gracious neighbors of the world:

Then the King will say to those at his right hand, "Come, O blessed of my Father, inherit the kingdom prepared for you from the foundation of the world; for I was hungry and you gave me food, I was thirsty and you gave me drink, I was a stranger and you welcomed me, I was naked and you clothed

---

[3] *Black Theology and Black Power*, p. 38.

119

me, I was sick and you visited me, I was in prison and you came to me. . . . Truly, I say to you, as you did it to one of the least of these my brethren, you did it to me."

(Matt. 25:34-36, 40)

The apostle Paul sees the very mystery of the incarnation unveiled in the image of Jesus as the gracious neighbor. "Have this mind among yourselves, which you have in Christ Jesus, who, though he was in the form of God, did not count equality with God a thing to be grasped, but emptied himself and became obedient unto death, even death on the cross." (Phil. 2:5-8) As that truth has been expressed in various "humiliation" or "kenotic" Christologies, it has often been associated with mythical notions which are hardly credible to us today. It has been interpreted to mean that Jesus, in an act of voluntary condescension, divested himself of such divine attributes as omnipotence and omniscience in order to make himself human; that he who had been God changed himself into a man. We must surely agree with D. M. Baillie that such an interpretation "seems more like a pagan story of metamorphosis than like the Christian doctrine of Incarnation." [4]

The "emptying" of which Paul speaks is rather the "self-emptying" of a love which gives itself utterly to men in their extremity. It is the rejection of the temptation to "play god" in relation to other men instead of playing the part of the gracious neighbor. Paradoxically, Jesus' refusal to lord it over men on the assumption of "an equality with God" qualified him pre-eminently to be a unique disclosure of the very essence of God as self-sacrificing love. His willingness to be the gracious neighbor even "unto death" made him (to use Tillich's phrase) utterly transparent to the ground of his being, God. In the "com-

[4] *God Was in Christ,* pp. 96-97.

plete orientation of human being in the experience of Jesus as one whose only concern is for others," in his "freedom from self maintained to the point of death," [5] men were able to see through to the loving heart of God himself. In this "man for others," in whose life and death unconditional love found such consistent expression, they had a sense of being in touch with the hidden source and ground of their very being.

One of the most revealing pictures of Jesus as the gracious neighbor is that dramatic foot-washing incident in the gospels in which he scandalized his disciples by a self-abasing demonstration of his solicitude for their need (John 13:3-16). In performing this humble chore usually reserved for the lowest class of slaves, Jesus shocked them into a re-evaluation of their understanding of his Lordship. His is a Lordship which does not express itself in "lording it over us," but in graciously stooping to serve us. We see Jesus truly when we see him, not as a king, but as a slave—or better still—when we allow his sovereignty to claim our imagination and loyalty through his servant-hood. The symbol of his office is not the monarch's scepter, but the servant's towel.

> The Kingdoms of the Earth go by
> In purple and in gold;
> They rise, they triumph, and they die,
> And all their tale is told.
>
> One Kingdom only is divine,
> One banner triumphs still,
> Its King a servant, and its sign
> A gibbet on a hill.

That "gibbet on a hill" is a perpetual reminder to us of what it costs to be the gracious neighbor. It isn't just a

[5] Bonhoeffer, *Prisoner for God*, p. 179.

matter of helping little old ladies across the street, or being "nice" to Negroes. For Jesus, being the "man for others" led inexorably to the pain and dereliction of the Cross. It led to alienation, misunderstanding, betrayal, suffering, and death.

We need to be careful not to assume, however, that Jesus pursued suffering as an end in itself. The Christ who prayed agonizingly in Gethsemane, "Father, if thou art willing, remove this cup from me," (Luke 22:42) should disabuse us of any such view. It is a monstrous distortion to make Jesus out as a masochist. Unfortunately, the example of too many Christians who find it easy to succumb to a "martyr complex" in the service of their Lord, has lent credence to such a misunderstanding. Jesus loved life as much as any of us. But he was prepared to run the risks of a life-style dominated by a radical love for his fellowmen. And such love is always supremely vulnerable to hurt and suffering.

In the image of the gracious neighbor, who is at the same time the "suffering servant," the church has through the ages found the central clue to the redemptive significance of Christ for the world. That is why the Cross has always been the main focus of Christian devotion. That image has, of course, often been grievously distorted by supernaturalistic schemes of salvation which depict the passion and death of Christ as the focal elements in a cosmic transaction concluded between God and Christ, or God and Satan. Such atonement theories, which make Christ's suffering into the pre-condition of God's forgiveness and reconciliation in accordance with the terms of a pre-arranged plan of salvation, is as incredible to us today as it is offensive.

This is not to say that Paul's great affirmation of faith that "God was in Christ reconciling the world to himself" (II Cor. 5:19) lies today beyond the limits of our credence.

It is still possible to see in the suffering and death of the Gracious Neighbor the searing mystery of a divine love which judges us, claims us, and accepts us. "God is both hidden and revealed in the suffering of Jesus. He is hidden in the mystery of love's burden, its vulnerability to misunderstanding, its initial powerlessness which becomes powerfully redemptive. God is revealed in Jesus's suffering because in him suffering is the authentic expression and communication of love." [6] "We know the love of God in this, that while we were yet sinners, Christ died for us." (Rom. 5:8) It is this conviction of the suffering love of God in Christ, mediated above all through the drama of his Cross, that somehow frees us to accept ourselves, and therefore to accept others, because we know that God accepts us in spite of our unacceptability. Thus we are liberated to be our true selves, to give ourselves in love for the neighbor, to live the life of the "man for others."

It is a tragic fact that the Cross, historically the symbol of Christ's ignominious rejection and costly servanthood, has in our day been so cheapened and trivialized that it serves as little more than the badge of membership in a respectable religious in-group. Seldom does it draw men powerfully and move them deeply. Albert Camus has caught the irony of this state of affairs in the concluding episode of his novel *The Stranger*. Meursault, a thoroughly alienated young man, is on trial for his life for the senseless shooting of an Arab for no apparent reason whatever. He is so estranged from life and society that he refuses to cooperate with the proceedings of the court or mount any kind of defense on his own behalf. The magistrate, driven to sheer exasperation by his behavior, takes a silver crucifix from a filing cabinet and waves it ostentatiously in the

[6] Daniel Day Williams, *The Spirit and the Forms of Love* (New York: Harper & Row, 1968), p. 167.

face of the defendant, while professing his own belief in God and declaring that "even the worst of sinners could obtain forgiveness of Him." Quite unmoved, Meursault can think only of the heat and the buzzing flies. The magistrate, "limp and dejected" at not being able to provoke any sort of response, concludes sadly: "Never in all my experience have I known a soul so case-hardened as yours. . . . All the criminals who have come before me until now wept when they saw this symbol of our Lord's sufferings." [7]

Camus's point is clear. The cross cannot be rehabilitated as a credible symbol, capable of evoking tears of recognition and repentance, as long as we are content simply to wave it in the faces of our "case-hardened" contemporaries. The skeptics of our age still say with the doubting Thomas: "Unless I see in his hands the print of the nails, and place my finger in the mark of the nails, and place my hand in his side, I will not believe." (John 20:25) Only the stigmata of the gracious neighbor, the marks of a costly human ministry, have the power to restore the waning credibility of the Cross.

The Joyous Revolutionary

Many readers may have followed our discussion of the meaning of Christ for today up until this point without experiencing any undue strain on their credulity. The chances are, however, that the heading of this section will produce in some an acute wrenching of the imagination. They can make some kind of sense of the picture of Christ as the gracious neighbor. But in the same breath to clothe him with the image of the revolutionary seems utterly out of keeping with the Christ they have been

[7] (New York: Alfred A. Knopf, 1946), pp. 84-87.

taught to believe in. After all, do not the suffering servant and the revolutionary conjure up images which, on the face of it, are bound to be incongruous and incompatible?

If these two images clash in the Christian consciousness today, it was not always so. We find it easy to forget that New Testament Christians were hailed before magistrates for being revolutionaries. In the book of Acts it is reported that "Jason and some of the brethren" were dragged before the city authorities and accused of "acting against the decrees of Caesar, saying that there is another king, Jesus." "These men who have turned the world upside down have come here also." (Acts 17:6-7) What is that but the familiar complaint of beleaguered establishments blaming their troubles on outside agitators! In the sixteenth century, let us not forget, the Peasant's Revolt and the revolutionary activity of the Anabaptists were Christian movements, fueled by Christian ideas and Christian slogans.

We must be quick to acknowledge, however, that this has not represented the dominant strain of historical Christianity. By and large, the church has stood out in history as a conservative and antirevolutionary force, the benign custodian of the status quo. Fearful of losing its place of privilege in the established order, it has been reluctant to identify with movements dedicated to bringing about fundamental social change. It has been the same old story of the chaplain in the Prince's palace, always nervous about the peasants at the gate. Throughout history Christians have been all too ready to appeal to passages like Romans 13 and I Peter 2 as justification for an unquestioning obedience to political tyrannies and a blanket discouragement of all revolutionary movements. Even Martin Luther felt constrained by these passages to give his support to the ruthless suppression of the Peasant's Revolt by the German nobles. In our own time, similar

125

theological justification was given by German Christians for their acquiescence in the diabolical crimes of the Hitler regime. More recently, there have been hosts of "silent majority" Christians in our own land who have applauded, in the name of "law and order," the reckless and brutal slaying of protesting students on our university campuses.

"Revolution," says Colin Morris, "is biblical faith's illegitimate child, who left home because the Church refused to acknowledge paternity." [8] It is the supreme tragedy of Christian history that the revolutionary impulses sired by the Christian faith have had to migrate out of the church and find a home elsewhere—and not always under the best of auspices. Christians who professedly worship a God who promises "a new heaven and a new earth," have been content to major on heavenly matters, leaving the struggle for a "new earth" to secular revolutionaries, humanists, and Marxists.

There are, however, signs emerging today that Christians are again finding their place in the revolutionary vanguard of a new world. In Latin America, for example, the Roman Catholic Church, long allied with landed aristocracies and military juntas, is voluntarily giving up its traditional privileges and giving away its landholdings for the benefit of the poor. In a recent statement on the stance of the church in a revolutionary situation, sixteen bishops of the Third World declared: "Christians and their pastors should know how to recognize the hand of the Almighty in those events that from time to time put down the mighty from their thrones and raise up the humble, send away the rich empty-handed, and fill the hungry with good things." [9] Camilo Torres, the guerrilla priest of Colombia, and Eduardo Mondlane, the leader

[8] *Unyoung—Uncolored—Unpoor*, p. 15.
[9] *New Theology No. 6*, p. 243. Cf. Luke 1:52-53.

of the Mozambique National Liberation Front, were both passionately dedicated Christians before they became victims of political assassination. As for those in our own country, time would fail to tell of Father James Groppi, Martin Luther King, Caesar Chavez, the Berrigan brothers, the Catonsville 9, the Milwaukee 14, and unnumbered anonymous revolutionary prophets who, like their biblical counterparts canonized in the book of Hebrews, "enforced justice, received promises . . . won strength out of weakness . . . suffered mocking and scourging, and even chains and imprisonment," and of whom it can also be said, "the world was not worthy" (Heb. 11:32-38).

What are we to say of these modern Christian revolutionaries? Are they to be dismissed as dangerous troublemakers and disturbers of the peace? Or is it possible that they have a mandate from a revolutionary Christ? Harvey Cox ventures the judgment that "the only man who can save the world today must be a mixture of the saint and the revolutionary." [10] If that be the case, then we must get about the business of wedding the terms "Christian" and "revolutionary," which have for too long been divorced in our Christian vocabulary. The Christian imagination must learn how to hold together in a mutually fruitful tension the images of the gracious neighbor and the joyous revolutionary.

Our reading of the gospels has been for so long conditioned by an establishment psychology that we can discern only with great difficulty the revolutionary dimensions in the picture they give us of Jesus. For one thing, we have difficulty seeing him as possessing the personal characteristics which would equip him to be a revolutionary. It takes a concerted effort of the imagination to break through the

[10] *Feast of Fools*, p. 117.

pious caricature of the "gentle Jesus, meek and mild" and make contact with him as the man he really was. For all his gentleness and compassion, for all his childlike simplicity and remarkable sensitivity to persons, Jesus was no "dewy-eyed sentimentalist who caroled about love because the harsher side of life was a closed book to him." [11] He was a man whose eyes could flash with anger and whose whole being could surge with indignation at the sight of exploitation and injustice. He was a man capable of the most vitriolic rhetoric and merciless satire, when faced with religious hypocrisy and opportunism. "Woe to you, scribes and Pharisees, hypocrites! for you are like whitewashed tombs, which outwardly appear beautiful, but within they are full of dead men's bones and all uncleanness." (Matt. 23:27) James Forman delivering his "Black Manifesto" in Riverside Church could hardly have outdone that!

Any fair reading of the gospels should convince us that Jesus was not a man averse to conflict and confrontation, or unequipped to deal with it. Nietzche's famous attack on Jesus as a man lacking in vital power and the ability to cope with conflict and opposition, who always chose the way of passive nonresistance, has no real support from the gospels. In answering that attack, Karl Jaspers has this to say: "In the Gospels one meets Jesus as an elemental power, no less clear in its hardness and aggressiveness than in those elements of infinite mildness. . . . It does not work to make of Jesus a patient, soft, loving figure, and even less to make of him a nervous, unresisting man." [12]

Another problem that many people have with the notion of a revolutionary Christ is their inability to see him

[11] Morris, *Unyoung—Uncolored—Unpoor*, p. 124.
[12] Quoted in W. Pannenberg, *Jesus—God and Man*, p. 236.

functioning in a political role or setting. Did he not say, "My kingdom is not of this world"? (John 18:36) Was his gospel not a spiritual one rather than a political one? How then can we make him fit the image of the social and political revolutionary?

Let it be freely granted that the primary focus of Jesus' message, at least as far as we are able to reconstruct it from the testimony of the early church, was on the inner revolution which must take place in men's hearts. It was a call to thoroughgoing repentance and faith in God in view of the immanence of the coming kingdom. It was a call to an inner change of heart so radical that it could be fittingly called a "new birth," a transformation of personal lifestyle so sweeping that it could be characterized as nothing less than a foretaste in the here and now of the "eternal life" to come. It needs also to be acknowledged that the social and political ramifications of this inner spiritual revolution are seldom mentioned in the gospels. This is the case for two reasons: partly no doubt because of the expectation of the immanent arrival of the kingdom (later proved to be mistaken) which precluded the necessity for Christians to assume long-term political responsibilities; and partly because, in the situation of an occupied country ruled by a tyrannical foreign power, there was little opportunity for significant political action. We can assume that he operated in a situation roughly comparable to present-day Czechoslovakia, where any independent political activity has to be highly secretive and carried on in an underground manner.

The force of these considerations must be recognized and given its due weight. On the one hand, we miss the real Jesus just as surely when we portray him exclusively in the role of the revolutionary political activist as when we portray him as the teacher of a purely spiritual, other-worldly gospel. On the other hand, however, there is no question that the inner spiritual revolution he proclaimed has profoundly revolutionary consequences for the way men live in the *polis*, and the way they order their political and social institutions. And there is no escaping the obvious political impact of his own public career as recorded in the gospel.

A premonition of Jesus' revolutionary challenge to the political powers-that-be is embedded even in the stories about his birth. Whatever its historical accuracy, Matthew's account of Herod's slaughter of the innocents is clearly meant to carry the impression that Jesus' coming constituted a threat to the security of the established order. G. K. Chesterton's comment on the significance of this story is highly suggestive: "There is in this buried divinity an idea of undermining the world; of shaking the towers and palaces from below even as Herod the great king felt that earthquake under him and swayed with his swaying palace." [13]

I have already had occasion to mention the charter of Jesus' messianic mission with which he launched his public career in a sermon in the synagogue at Nazareth. The planks in his platform were these: "good news to the poor," "release to the captives and recovering of sight to the blind," "liberty to those who are oppressed" (Luke 4:18-19). Surely the manifesto of a freedom fighter, if there ever was one! By the time that sermon was over, a pious congregation of Sabbath worshipers had been transformed into a lynch mob. They ended up by running him out of the city and trying to throw him over a cliff. Here is the classic story of what happens when a hometown boy stops "preaching the gospel" and starts meddling with unorthodox and revolutionary social ideas.

[13] *The Everlasting Man* (New York: Doubleday & Co., 1955), pp. 209-10.

There are many incidents in the gospels which must have branded Jesus as a dangerous revolutionary in the eyes of the authorities. There is the attempt by the crowd, on the occasion of the feeding of the five thousand, to make him king by force. There is his continual fraternizing with the riffraff, the social outcasts, the "street people" of his day. There are the recurring jibes at the rich and the powerful. At the end, there is the elaborately contrived "demonstration march" into Jerusalem, which we celebrate on Palm Sunday as a purely religious event, but which, whatever Jesus' own intentions, was bound to be construed by the public and the ruling authorities as a bid for a political following.

Finally, there is his climactic challenge of the religious-political establishment in his cleansing of the Temple. This personalization of the judgment of God against the exploiters of the poor by creating a scandalous public disturbance in the very precincts of the religio-political power structure—this was the last straw. He had to go! There is hardly room for doubt that he was put to death for his revolutionary activities and because he was considered a political threat to those who held the reins of power. The instrument of his execution was the one reserved for those found guilty of insurrection. And there is a good possibility that the criminals who shared his final hours of agony were members of a band of revolutionary Zealots, an organized guerrilla movement dedicated to the overthrow of the Roman tyranny.[14]

Whatever else Jesus was, it is hard to avoid the conclusion that he was a revolutionary. But he was a revolutionary with a difference. We are justified in seeing him, I

[14] A New Testament scholar from England, Professor S. G. F. Brandon, has recently advanced a carefully documented thesis that Jesus was much closer to the Zealots than previous scholarship has indicated. See *Jesus and the Zealots* (Manchester: Manchester University Press, 1967).

think, as a model of the authentic revolutionary, which stands in judgment against so much that goes on in the name of revolution today. The key to the difference lies in the qualifier "joyous."

Too often revolutionaries are somber Puritan types, compulsively dedicated fanatics, humorless and loveless characters prepared to sacrifice every human value to their burning revolutionary obsession. Such a revolutionary is described in a pamphlet called *The Revolutionary Catechism* written in 1868: "The revolutionary is a dedicated man. He has no interest, no business, no emotions, no attachment, no property, not even a name. In his innermost depths he has broken all ties with the social order. He knows but one science, that of destruction. The tender sentiments of family, friendship, love, and gratitude must be subjugated to the single cold passion of the revolutionary cause." [15] That is the picture of a bloodless cipher and not a real man! When such men as this make a revolution, it is bound to be profoundly dehumanizing and nihilistic in its results. Harvey Cox rightly detects a tendency in this direction in many of the members of the "New Left": "The flaw in the new militants is that in their passion to live in a more human world they sometimes fail to relish those first fruits that are present today. They lack a festive élan. Earnest, committed, even zealous, they often suffer from a fatal humorlessness. Their 'no' is so much louder than their 'yes' that they seem to skirt very close to the borders of nihilism." [16]

I am proposing as an antidote to the grim moralism and fanatical nihilism of many of today's revolutionaries the image of Christ as the joyous revolutionary, who in pursuing his vision of a world remade never ceases to be at the

[15] Quoted in Morris, *Unyoung—Uncolored—Unpoor*, p. 156.
[16] *Feast of Fools*, p. 119.

same time the very incarnation of the gracious neighbor. What does he look like in this role? Certainly he does not cut the figure of a Bar Kochba, the fanatical Zealot, or of a John the Baptist, the preacher of repentance. He never made the mistake, as we so often do, of confusing serious-ness with solemnity. He never regarded it as his calling to proclaim to his contemporaries "the importance of being earnest." Indeed he seemed to go out of his way to demon-strate that "the deep earnestness of love for suffering man can be joined with the cheerful play of faith in God." [17] There was about him the infectious quality of *hilaritas,* the joyous certainty of a man who knows that the future is secured in spite of all the evidence to the contrary. His was the radical posture of life under grace. That is why he could run the risks he did. That is why he defied re-spectable conventions, poked fun at would-be demigods, took time out to attend dinner parties, and generally gained for himself the reputation of being "a glutton and a winebibber."

The followers of John the Baptist were appalled that Jesus did not require his disciples to fast as they and the Pharisees did. "Can the wedding guests mourn," Jesus said to them, "as long as the bridegroom is still with them?" (Matt. 9:15) So he continued to celebrate the heavenly banquet of the faithful right down to the very eve of his death. The Last Supper, which took place in the very shadow of the Cross, was far from being a dolorous event. It was concluded by the singing of the great Free-dom Song of the Jewish nation (Ps. 114–18) and a pointed reminder of the certainty of God's coming kingdom: "This is my blood of the covenant, which is poured out for many. Truly, I say to you, I shall not drink again of the fruit of the vine until that day when I drink it new in the

---

[17] Moltmann, *Religion, Revolution, and the Future,* p. 147.

kingdom of God" (Mark 14:24-25). Jesus was the joyous revolutionary right up to the end.

Christ the revolutionary points beyond himself to the God who is in the business of making revolutions on the earth. The God and Father of our Lord Jesus Christ is the same God who summoned Jeremiah to collaborate in his ongoing revolutionary activity: "See, I have set you this day over nations and over kingdoms, to pluck up and to break down, to destroy and to overthrow, to build and to plant" (Jer. 1:10). He is, as we have noted earlier, that dynamic power at work in history which makes for humanizing change. As the power of an ever renewed future, he is the hidden agitator behind every revolution which lifts the yoke of oppression from the bodies and the spirits of men. Through Christ he continues to call us to participation in those revolutions which kindle in men's breasts the spark of freedom, hope, and human dignity.

The Invincible Pioneer

There is something about the image of the pioneer that still fascinates us, even though the West has long since been won, and the first trails through the trackless wildernesses have long since been blazed. Perhaps it is more than romanticism which stirs our imagination when we hear the tales of those intrepid pioneers of frontier America, who pushed forward into the infinite spaces of an uncharted land and staked their claim on territories hitherto unknown and inaccessible to man. The recent exploits of our moon pioneers have struck a similar responsive chord deep within the human psyche. There seems to be an eternal restlessness in the spirit of man which impels him toward the frontiers and lures him ever onward over the next horizon.

If this restless frontier spirit is intrinsic to man's nature, what is he going to do as our little "spaceship earth" be-comes more and more crowded, his horizons become more and more contracted, and finally there are no new frontiers left to lure and beckon him onward? Jürgen Moltmann has suggested, in a provocative preface to his 1967–68 American lectures, that we must be prepared in our day to exchange the frontiers of space for the frontiers of time. "It is no longer the open land which invites and challenges us, but the open future." [18] Today man's drive for freedom and a new life must be expressed not in spatial migration to a "new world" but in pioneering a "new age," opening up a new future by political and social transformation of the space he now occupies.

It is in this context that the image of Christ as the in-vincible pioneer may be able again to speak powerfully to our generation. In the past Christians have often spoken of Christ the pioneer in mythical language. But it is en-tirely possible to restate their central conviction in secular terms. For the writer of the book of Hebrews, the images of Christ as the gracious neighbor and the invincible pioneer were inseparable: "It was fitting that he, for whom and by whom all things exist, in bringing many sons to glory, should make the *pioneer* of their salvation perfect through suffering" (Heb. 2:10). "Let us run with persever-ance the race that is set before us, looking to Jesus the *pioneer* and perfecter of our faith, who for the joy that was set before him endured the cross, despising the shame, and is seated at the right hand of the throne of God." (Heb. 12:1-2)

We should not allow that myth about Jesus, perched somewhere on a celestial throne as God's right-hand man, to blind us to the powerful affirmation that the early Chris-tians were making through this kind of pictorial imagery.

[18] *Ibid.*, p. xv.

They were simply witnessing to the exhilarating fact that they had found in the man Jesus the pioneer who had decisively broken open their future, foreshadowing the true humanity which was potentially theirs, and disclosing the very drift and destiny of history itself. "The life of Jesus, they discovered, was a life in which the expected limits of human existence constantly were being transcended. In him they met authority, truth, wholeness; through him they were given the assurance of the way and in him they encountered a life which transcended even the boundary of death." [19] His brief public ministry of three years, culminating in his death and resurrection, was for them more than simply the career of an unusually exemplary individual. It constituted for them, though in a far more ultimate sense, what space-pioneer Neil Armstrong claimed for his first step on the moon—"a giant leap forward for all mankind." It was a breakthrough into the future which would change forever the environment in which men were to live, opening up new horizons of hope never before envisaged by the human imagination. The excitement of the millions of people around the world who watched man's landing on the moon via Telstar was mild in comparison to the hope-charged exhilaration of those first witnesses to Christ's pioneering breakthrough into the future.

The apostle Paul tried to express this breathtaking vision of Christ's pioneering work for mankind in his doctrine of the "second Adam." As the "second Adam" he pioneered a new way of being human, a way to which all men are called, but from which the whole race of the "first Adam" has become diverted by an assortment of evil powers of its own making. "What mankind could not do, this man did. In Adam all died, but in this second Adam is new

[19] Williams, *Faith in a Secular Age,* p. 79.

life to be found. Here is the first of a new race. He loosened the grip of the powers on the future. He pushed open the door. Now we can go through! . . . Because he pioneered, we can follow." [20]

As Paul Lehmann has pointed out, the doctrine of the "second Adam" requires the doctrine of the "second Advent" for its completion. It is obvious, of course, that the notion of Christ's second coming must undergo extensive demythologizing to gain any kind of credibility today. Lehmann makes a beginning in this direction in the following statement of its meaning: "It simply means that Jesus Christ who, in and with his historical existence inaugurated a new age and a new humanity, will come again, as the New Testament puts it, 'with power and glory,' to consummate what he has begun. 'Power and glory' denote the final and radical transvaluation of the whole created and historical order of which the second Adam and the new humanity are a guarantee and foretaste." [21]

Only the incurably literal-minded can think of this "coming again" in terms of a Christophany, with Jesus coming in on a cloud to the sound of celestial trumpets. Some, a trifle less literalistic, would like to update the imagery, and depict it as the sort of event which could be flashed around the globe via Telstar and reported by Walter Cronkite. But not many today will be satisfied with that kind of science fiction interpretation. If we are to make any sense out of the second advent at all, we must see it as an expression of the hope that ultimately the ambiguities of history will be resolved, the human family will come to its true maturity in the kingdom of God, and what we have seen of the "new humanity" in the person of Jesus

[20] Gabriel Fackre, *The Rainbow Sign* (Grand Rapids: Eerdmans Publishing Co., 1969), p. 54.
[21] *Ethics in a Christian Context*, p. 122.

Christ will be unmistakably and invincibly regnant in a "new heaven and a new earth."

There have been those who have attempted to translate this hope in the final victory of Christ into daring metaphysical visions which see in Christ the driving force of the whole cosmic process. Many have been fascinated by Teilhard de Chardin's bold vision of a universe in the process of Christogenesis, with all reality converging towards Christ as the Omega Point of the world's evolution, drawn by his attractive power to its consummation in God.[22] While not everyone may be able to follow him in these breathtaking flights of the metaphysical imagination, there is no question that his portrayal of the cosmic Christ has affinities with the faith of many of the early Christians. They expressed it in the most extravagant language imaginable: "I am the Alpha and the Omega, the first and the last, the beginning and the end" (Rev. 22:13). "He is the image of the invisible God, the first-born of all creation. . . . He is before all things, and in him all things hold together." (Col. 1:15, 17)

How do you explain these incredibly confident expectations for the future? How can Christians entertain such audacious hopes for the outcome of history, such colossal optimism for the human race? Here we must acknowledge, however difficult it may be for us moderns to assimilate, that, for the early Christians, the anchor of their hope, the fulcrum of their world-sweeping vision of the future, was the event of the death and resurrection of Jesus. There is no question that the resurrection boggles the imagination and defies the belief capacity of modern secular men perhaps more than any other Christian affirmation. And yet it is impossible to eliminate it from the logic of Christian hope. Here more than anywhere else the demand for

[22] Cf. *The Divine Milieu* (New York: Harper & Row, 1960).

credibility may tempt us to remove an indispensable linch-pin from the structure of Christian belief.

Gordon Kaufman has properly observed that the resur-rection-event is much more crucial to Christian faith than the alleged virgin birth: "Whereas the latter was a theo-logically crude attempt to explain something already be-lieved in—that Jesus was the Son of God—*the resurrection was the event in which this belief itself was born. . . . There would have been no Christian faith had this event not hap-pened.*" [23] As a consequence of this event, the disciples, thoroughly demoralized and disillusioned following the crucifixion, were infused with a new and militant hope—"we have been born anew to a living hope through the resurrection of Jesus Christ from the dead" (I Pet. 1:3). Something had happened which they interpreted as God's vindication of Jesus and his mission. Whatever it was, it reassured them that the kingdom which he had an-nounced as immanent was in fact being inaugurated. It confirmed their badly battered faith that he was indeed their invincible pioneer who had opened up their future and provided them with the "first fruits" of God's "new age."

If something called the resurrection had not happened, then the life of Jesus would have ended in heartbreaking tragedy. We would be faced with something truly in-credible—a church which has survived the rigors of the centuries founded on the death of a tragic hero. The very nerve of the Christian faith would be cut. The claim that Christ is the invincible pioneer of faith could be written off as little more than a way of "whistling to keep our courage up." "If Christ has not been raised," says Paul, "then our preaching is in vain and your faith is in vain. . . . If Christ has not been raised, your faith is futile and you are still in your sins" (I Cor. 15:14, 17).

[23] *Systematic Theology: A Historicist Perspective,* pp. 414-15.

I do not propose to indulge here in the largely unfruit-ful speculations concerning the mechanics of the resurrec-tion, with which theologians have often preoccupied them-selves. Here is one of those points where Bonhoeffer's caveat against pressing the question "how?" in relation to the mystery of Christ is particularly appropriate. In any case, we are not here talking about something amenable to clinical examination or objective proof. That is why the bit of graffiti scratched on the wall of a university building, "There'll be no Easter this year—We've found the body!" should cause us no great consternation. Whether we choose to align ourselves with Ronald Gregor Smith when he de-clares that "we may freely say that the bones of Jesus lie somewhere in Palestine";[24] or with Gordon Kaufman, who believes that the resurrection was a series of "halluci-nations" through which "God was acting to bring his king-dom powerfully into human history";[25] or with the apostle Paul, who speculates imaginatively about something he calls a "spiritual body" (I Cor. 15:35-50); in no case do we get much beyond the realm of pious conjecture. About the only thing we can affirm with reasonable certainty is that the resurrection was *not* a physical resuscitation of Jesus' body. Not only is that ruled out by the nature of the appearances to Paul and the disciples, but by the fact that it leaves us, as Tillich has said, with "the absurd question . . . as to what happened to the molecules which comprise the corpse of Jesus of Nazareth."[26]

As to whether Christ lives on in some kind of "non-molecular" or "spiritual" body is a purely speculative point, not of vital interest to Christian faith. What is of in-terest, and indeed of ultimate concern, is that the reality which surfaced in history in the person and ministry of the

[24] *Secular Christianity* (New York: Harper & Row, 1966), p. 103.
[25] *Systematic Theology: A Historicist Perspective*, pp. 424-25.
[26] *Systematic Theology* II, 156.

pre-resurrection Jesus did not come to an ignominious end with his death on the cross. What faith insists on establishing is that Christ, as a consequence of the resurrection, has a future. It sees the resurrection as God's way of accrediting Jesus' vision of the new humanity and the transfigured world to which his words and his deeds, his suffering and his death, had pointed. It finds in that resurrection-event the assurance that the one who confronted men in his lifetime as the gracious neighbor and the joyous revolutionary is still at work in the world in those roles, only now authenticated by God himself as the pioneer of a new race, invincibly guaranteeing the world's future as the future of God.

At this point we must be careful not to fall into the pitfall of a theology of glory in which the triumph of Easter simply swallows up the suffering of Good Friday, and the ultimate fulfillment is prematurely celebrated as present fact. The fact is that, between the resurrection and the *parousia,* the world continues to writhe in the agony of unfulfillment, even though it has received the first fruits of its final redemption. History continues to inscribe in its records the horrors of man's inhumanity to man. Infamies like My Lai and tragedies like Kent State continue to document the intransigence of evil and suffering in the human story. Easter has not changed all that. It has run up a flag of hope, to be sure, but it has not yet produced "the new heaven and the new earth." If resurrection-talk is to be credible in an age so massively scarred as ours by conflict, suffering, and tragedy, it must be grounded unmistakably in a theology of the cross. What this implies for our understanding of the risen Christ has been admirably expressed by Carl Braaten:

The risen Christ is present in our not-yet-fulfilled world in cruci-form. The resurrection was not for Jesus an exit from our brutal world into heavenly bliss above. It is not the story of how one man made it through enemy lines and now waits peacefully on the other side to see if others will get through. The first witnesses identified the risen Jesus by the marks of his crucifixion. The body of the risen Jesus can be identified by us in the bruised and bleeding body of mankind with which he identified himself.[27]

The resurrection indeed assured Jesus of a future. But it is a future which does not abandon the earth on which his cross was raised. It is a future which includes us and our embattled world, struggling for human dignity, freedom, justice, and brotherhood. It is a future which has some recognizable continuity with the past. There is a sense in which Christ has gone on ahead of us as the invincible pioneer of an as yet (for us) unrealized future. There is another sense in which he stands with us as our contemporary; still our gracious neighbor sharing in the sufferings and injustices of the present; and still the joyous revolutionary participating in our revolt against them.

The three images of Christ which we have been seeking to illuminate are thus brought together in revealing focus in his cross and resurrection. This double event is the decisive climax of God's liberating action in history. It represents both God's *identification with* and his *protest against* the sufferings of history. Moltmann writes illuminatingly about the revolutionary implications of such an idea:

When we understand the cross of Christ . . . as an expression of *real* human affliction, then the resurrection of Christ achieves the significance of the true "protest" against human affliction. Consequently, the missionary proclamation of the cross of the Resurrected One is not an opium of the people which intoxicates and incapacitates, but the ferment of new freedom. It leads to the awakening of that revolt which, in the "power of

[27] *The Future of God,* p. 83.

the resurrection" (as Paul expresses it), follows the categorical imperative to overthrow all conditions in which man is a being who labors and is heavily laden.[28]

If that statement captures an essential meaning of the resurrection, then one can understand why it is almost impossible for comfortable, affluent, insulated, middle-class Christians to celebrate Easter in its full New Testament significance. One has to *feel* the pain and dereliction of the cross in order to enter fully into the experience of the resurrection as God's "protest" against human alienation and suffering. Perhaps that is why black Christians are more apt to find the resurrection a credible article of faith than most white Christians.

This insight was borne in on me with overwhelming force on a visit a couple of years ago to a meeting of Operation Breadbasket in one of the large black churches of Chicago. It was the Saturday before Easter and the first anniversary of the martyrdom of Martin Luther King. As I sat through that four-hour service in the company of several thousand others, I became increasingly aware of the fact that I was participating not so much in a memorial service as a victory celebration. Never have I seen a people so delirious with joy and so exultant with hope. Here the resurrection was real because the cross was also real. If anyone doubted it, he had only to listen to the message sent by Dick Gregory from his cell in the Cook County jail, or the reports of the cynical exploitation of the poor on Chicago's south side, or Jesse Jackson's moving rehearsal of the events of King's assassination.

But if these people knew the suffering and humiliation of the cross, they also knew the power of the resurrection. Nothing less could sustain their defiant protest against

[28] "Toward a Political Hermeneutics of the Gospel" in *New Theology No. 6*, p. 79.

those enslaving powers which would degrade their humanity and demean their spirit. They had got a whiff of God's freedom, a piece of God's liberating action. And nothing could persuade them that their fallen leader did not live on in that movement of emancipation against which the powers of death itself could not prevail. What could be more natural than that they should see him as the living incarnation of the gracious neighbor, the joyous revolutionary, and the invincible pioneer of their salvation, blazing new trails for freedom, justice, and human brotherhood?

Jesus Christ: Final or Provisional?

The foregoing identification of Martin Luther King as in some sense a real, contemporary embodiment of the crucified and risen Christ may, at first blush, seem altogether too bold (if not blasphemous) a claim to be credited seriously. Does it not put in jeopardy the finality of Christ and the sufficiency of his "once-for-all' sacrifice for the redemption of the human race? Does it not suggest that his saving work on the cross is not really completed after all, and that other "redeemers" are necessary to reconcile the world to its true destiny in God? And does this not contradict an important Christian claim that the redemption of the world has *already* been accomplished by Christ's work of reconciliation on the cross?

These objections echo much traditional Christian theology which has failed to maintain a proper balance between the "already" and the "not yet" of Christ's redemptive work. This is reflected in the tendency to conceive of redemption as a perfectly consummated once-for-all event rather than a continuing process. There is a valid and important sense, of course, in which what Christ did for men represents a once-for-all event. In that event God decisively demonstrated and enacted his love for men and opened up for them a radically new future in the new humanity embodied in Jesus Christ. That this happened in a real man in our historical past brands it as a once-for-all event which subsequent history cannot abrogate or change. In this sense, then, we can talk about the finality of Christ. The Christian will always take his bearings from this event, and because of it, history can never be the same again.

There is another sense, however, in which the work of Christ is not final, but provisional. The world still does not *look* redeemed, nor is it *in fact* redeemed. Christ's reconciling and liberating work was not completed in his death and resurrection two thousand years ago. It will not be completed until the tragic divisions which alienate men from one another, and produce family conflict and race hatred and fratricidal war, are healed once and for all. It will not be completed until men are actually freed from the inner and outer bondages forged by their pride and greed and selfishness. It will not be completed until men are united in the perfect community of God's love and "the kingdom of the world has become the kingdom of our Lord and of his Christ" (Rev. 11:15). Until that *eschaton* for which Christ has given us hope, he is present to us, not as the final Christ, but as the provisional Christ—the Christ who calls us to participate in his continued suffering and share in his unfinished work.

A christological triumphalism which makes too much of the "finished work" of Christ is a theological error which has had lamentable consequences in the history of the church. It has led to the kind of "cheap grace" which Bonhoeffer talked about, based on the assumption that the grace of God has been so perfectly and completely secured that we can ignore the demands of a costly discipleship. Even more tragic, it has fed the totalitarian pretensions of

145

a church which has made itself the exclusive repository of grace and salvation. Dorothee Sölle has made the charge, not without good reason, that it has been the doctrine of a "final Christ" which has produced the ugly history of anti-Semitism in the church.[29] If history is thought to have ended and the kingdom of God come in Christ, then there is no room for the Jew. A Polish Jew has said that whenever he hears the name "Christ" he immediately thinks of "pogroms." Surely the silent voices of millions of tragic victims of the gas chambers and concentration camps cry out for a re-examination of our theology at this point.

There are other people than the Jews, however, who stand to benefit from a revision of our notions about a "final Christ." As Miss Sölle has observed, "those who have the final Christ need no future." "But," she goes on to say, "a future is precisely what those who happen to be the underdogs and the also-rans at any given time need more than anything else. Their future is betrayed in the name of the final Christ, the very future which the provisional Christ keeps open for them." [30] Those who suffer the pain and anguish of an unfulfilled and unredeemed world can identify with a still suffering Christ who nevertheless points them to an open future; they cannot identify with a Christ who reigns in glory, out of touch with the continuing brutalities of history. And they certainly cannot identify with a triumphalist church, so busy celebrating the victory of Christ that it passes by on the other side when the victims of man's inhumanity to man come into view.

I must confess to a certain uneasiness in speaking of Christ as "provisional." Perhaps the word suggests too much the idea of a makeshift arrangement, something

[29] See *Christ the Representative,* pp. 107-12.
[30] *Ibid.,* p. 110.

necessarily surpassable. If this is what is meant, then Christ is not a reliable clue to our future or the future of God. It is precisely this, however, which Christian faith must, at all costs, affirm—that Jesus is genuinely anticipatory of the end and goal of history, of the consummation of the "new humanity." But it can make this claim of finality for Christ without foreclosing his future in history. It can do so without inhibiting new forms of Christ from emerging in the church and the world. For, after all, his significance for us lies, not so much in what he is, but what he points to as the pioneer of our salvation and the "first-fruits" of a new age.

If to speak about the "provisionality of Christ" is to say that he is utterly dependent on us for the completion of his mission, that he is prepared to risk the future by putting it in our hands, then it seems to me we have no option but to affirm it. To do otherwise is to reduce history to the inexorable unfolding of a predetermined divine plan in which human agency makes no real difference to a world in principle already redeemed.

Here we must take with the utmost seriousness our image of Christ as pioneer. The pioneer simply blazes the initial trail. He leaves for others coming after him the task of clearing the forests, cultivating the land, and building the cities. The role of the pioneer does not preclude, but rather invites, our making the same journey that he did. Christ as our pioneer does not substitute for us; his mission does not replace ours; his suffering and joy are not his alone, but ours as well. He is indeed the way, the truth, and the life. But he is the way "that throws light upon our way without restricting our freedom to search for still undiscovered ways." He is the truth "that holds the open door to ever new truth." He is the life "that keeps us growing to maturity without reducing our responsibility to seek for ever increasing sources of life beyond those yet known to us." [31]

Such a *provisional* finality in Christ treats us as sons and not as slaves. It puts us on the road to an open future and gives us a share in the making of history. It lays upon us the mandate to carry on the ministry of the gracious neighbor and the joyous revolutionary in our own broken and loveless world. It summons us to pioneer new ways of being human in the cities of men, even as we press forward in hope to the final city of God.

[31] Williams, *Faith in a Secular Age*, p. 77.

PART FOUR

TOWARD
A
NEW
HUMANITY

VI

CHRISTIAN EXISTENCE: A NEW WAY OF BEING HUMAN

The theological perspective which I have been sketching, it will have been noted, relies heavily on the word "human" and a variety of its cognates. I have used frequently such expressions as "authentic humanity," "true humanity," "new humanity," "dehumanizing structures," and "humanizing change." We have looked at the way in which God is characteristically at work in the world to create and to nurture our essential humanity and bring about authentic human community. We have seen the way in which Christ images and pre-figures the "new humanity" to which all men are called. It remains for us now to examine a little more closely the content of that "new humanity" towards which God's redemptive activity in history is aiming.

It must be acknowledged that when we say, with Paul Lehmann, that God is in the business of making and keeping life human, or when we identify salvation with the humanization of our history, we are using language which is sufficiently ambiguous as to produce possible confusion and misunderstanding. It is imperative, therefore, that any such confusion be dissipated by a clarification of what is meant by the theological usage of the word "human" and its many variants.

Roger Shinn has reminded us of the need to differentiate between the empirical and normative uses of this word: "Empirically speaking, the Nazi destruction of six million Jews was human. It was not done by inhuman tigers or impersonal computers. People—men and even women—did it. We can call it inhuman only if we have some evalua-

151

tion of what it is to be human." [1] In its empirical meaning, the word "human" designates anything that human beings do; and that, as we know, runs all the way from the saintly to the satanic. In its normative sense, the word implies an ideal of what man "ought" to be, or what in his "true" nature as created by God he is intended to be and capable of becoming. It is in this normative sense that it becomes meaningful to talk about battling the dehumanizing forces of history and working for the humanization of the social order.

If this way of speaking is to be illuminating, however, we must be clear as to the normative content of these terms. What freight of meaning do they carry which enables us to make concrete judgments about what is truly human and what is antihuman or dehumanizing in our day-to-day experience? To answer this question, we must try to describe in some detail the life-style, the new way of being human, implicit in the "new humanity" pioneered for us by Christ. For it is here, Christian faith affirms, that we find the ultimate norm of our humanity, in terms of which all our halting efforts to be truly human are judged.

Christian Existence as True Humanity

Christian existence (described variously in the New Testament as "life in Christ," "life in the Spirit," "salvation") is nothing other than the actualization in history of our true humanity. To describe the style and structure of Christian existence is simply to delineate a new way of being human which corresponds to man's true nature as a creature of God. Paul refers to it as that "mature man-

---

[1] *New Directions in Theology Today, Vol. VI. Man: The New Humanism* (Philadelphia: Westminster Press, 1968), pp. 165-66.

hood" which finds its paradigmatic image in "the measure of the stature of the fullness of Christ" (Eph. 4:12).

Here we must be on our guard against the common temptation to characterize the Christian life in religiously esoteric or superhuman terms. What goes into the making of a Christian is not an alien *addendum* to human life which transforms him into something other than a man. "Faith is not something added to man's being. It is not so to speak, a luxury reserved for those who are talented or demanding in matters of religion, which they only can or need afford. For the aim of faith is to bring man to his true humanity, to let him be the creature and son of God. . . . The believer, therefore, is not a superman, but true man." [2]

Bonhoeffer's experiences in a Nazi prison camp persuaded him of the inadequacy of the usual pietistic portrayal of the Christian life as a life apart from other men, marked by distinctive religious observances or ascetic practices. He was struck increasingly by the phoniness of those Christians who went out of their way to be "pious" or "churchy" in order to emphasize their difference from the common run of men. "The Christian is not a *homo religiosus*," he protested, "but a man, pure and simple, just as Jesus was a man." [3] On the basis of this presupposition, he went on to describe the life-style of the Christian in secular terms. Christian existence, as he saw it, is not a mode of living which is sterilized and insulated from worldly contact and contamination. It is a life of total responsiveness to, and immersion in, the problems, joys, and sufferings of the world. Such Christian worldliness is a far cry, of course, from the smug, self-indulgent

[2] Gerhard Ebeling, *The Nature of Faith* (Philadelphia: Fortress Press, 1961), p. 116.
[3] *Prisoner for God*, p. 168.

worldliness of the typical hedonist of our day. As Bonhoeffer defines it, it is "taking life in one's stride, with all its duties and problems, its successes and failures, its experiences and helplessness. It is in such a life that we throw ourselves in the arms of God and participate in his sufferings in the world and watch with Christ in Gethsemane. That is faith, that is *metanoia,* and that is what makes a man and a Christian." [4]

Jan M. Lochman, reflecting his experience as a Christian in Communist-dominated Czechoslovakia, shares Bonhoeffer's concern for a worldly Christian life style. He is fearful that Christianity is frequently discounted because it is associated in many people's minds with a certain dress or "uniform" which distracts them from seeing the authentic marks of the Christian life. "To be a Christian," according to this misleading image, "implies taking part in religious ceremonies, liturgical actions, pious usages, or self-denying exercises. Or one may interpret Christian faith in a moralistic, puritanical sense: the Christian 'does not smoke, or drink, or dance.' " [5] In order to steer clear of these spurious badges of identification, Czech Protestants have sought "*a civilian mode of life* for Christians—a *witness without religious uniform.*" [6] The true Christian is prepared to doff all religious uniforms which artificially separate him from his neighbors. "To the Jews he is like a Jew and to the Greeks like a Greek." "He is not a person who on principle always draws lines and guards them—one who is always different, a man whose heart beats to a rhythm different from that of his fellowmen. On the contrary, he is, in the full meaning of

[4] *Ibid.,* p. 169.
[5] *Church in a Marxist Society* (New York: Harper & Row, 1970), p. 71.
[6] *Ibid.,* p. 70.

the phrase, a *'con*temporary,' a man among men—a *civilian*." [7]

Does this mean, then, that there is nothing to distinguish the Christian from other men, that Christian existence is utterly lacking in any kind of visibility? For Kierkegaard, the answer is "yes." His "knight of faith" moved among men entirely "incognito." "Good Lord," Kierkegaard asks, "is this the man? Is it really he? Why, he looks like a tax-collector!" [8] Get him in a church with a crowd of nominal churchgoers, and there is absolutely no way of identifying him. "No heavenly glance or any other token of the incommensurable betrays him; if one did not know him, it would be impossible to distinguish him from the rest of the congregation, for his healthy and vigorous hymn-singing proves at the most that he has a good chest." [9]

We can agree wth Kierkegaard that the true Christian does not reveal himself by pious looks or lusty hymn-singing. This is hardly sufficient, however, to prove his point that Christian existence is a totally hidden phenomenon. If this were the case, if the Christian life bore no distinctive marks which witness to others of an authentically new way of being human, it would be hard to see how it would appeal to anyone as a particularly credible way of life.

As a matter of fact, the credibility of the Christian way of life has suffered enormously from the wrong kind of invisibility (which Kierkegaard himself exposed unmercifully). Christian existence has undergone such a process of cultural assimilation and dilution, that it has been turned into an indistinguishable duplicate of other forms of human life. The result has been, as the French theologian, Roger

[7] *Ibid.*, p. 72.
[8] "Fear and Trembling" in Robert Bretall, ed., *A Kierkegaard Anthology* (New York: Modern Library, 1946), p. 119.
[9] *Ibid.*, p. 120.

Mehl, has observed, that "the Christian has become Mr. Average Man, the ordinary Western man, undoubtedly recognizable in the practice of certain virtues (themselves ordinary) which he shares with many of his fellow citizens." [10] The churches are full of such culture-Christians who embrace Christianity as the symbol of belonging to an "okay" world, but whose basic life-style mirrors the values and prejudices of the wider society. In their case, Christian existence has been aborted by their lust for social approval and acceptance.

This cultural levelling of the Christian life-style to the common denominator of the socially respectable presents the church today with a yawning credibility gap. "These Christians must show me they are redeemed," cried Nietzsche, "before I will believe in their Redeemer." That is still pretty much the dilemma confronting the church. The situation cannot be remedied by calling more and more people into the religious fold. The problem will not be lessened by an evangelism which enrolls "thousands of statistical Christians to make their 'decision' for Christ— a form of Instant Religion which, apparently in a flash, transforms them from nominal sinners into socially respectable citizens." [11] We can begin to attack the problem only when we are able to show how Christian existence qualifies and transforms human life in such a way as to offer a credible and contagious alternative to other conventional ways of being human.

Enough has now been said to make it clear that, in stressing the continuity between Christian existence and general human existence, I do not mean to cancel out any real distinction between the two. Only now it should be somewhat clearer where the *real* distinction arises. It is

[10] *Images of Man* (Richmond: John Knox Press, 1965), p. 43.
[11] Pierre Berton, *The Comfortable Pew* (Toronto: McClelland and Stewart, 1965), p. 89.

a distinction *within* the realm of the human and *between* alternative ways of being human; it is not a distinction between a human and an essentially nonhuman (religious, otherworldly) mode of existence. Lochman's "civilian" Christian "stands where his neighbors stand, but he stands there as one who tries to remain faithful to his Lord. Here, then, begins the way of the Christian—in following Jesus, in believing, hoping, and loving. In the midst of unbelief, faith. In the midst of despair, hope. In the midst of hatred, love. When this is happening, the true distinction and the real witness comes to pass." [12] But it comes to pass, not as a calculated effort to be "peculiar" or different, but as the natural outcome of a fundamental orientation of life which produces a genuinely new way of being human.

For this new way of being human, we are not in a position to offer any precise blueprints. In a sense, we are dealing here with "a theology of a pilgrim journey which makes its own map as it goes." [13] To be sure, the apostle Paul points to some hallmarks of the Christian life when he lists the fruits of the Spirit as "love, joy, peace, patience, kindness, goodness, faithfulness, gentleness, self-control" (Gal. 5:22-23). But these are no more than random illustrations of the Christian life-style; they fall far short of providing us with a reliable and comprehensive road map for our Christian pilgrimage today.

In what follows, I shall attempt to specify something of the general structure of Christian existence by showing how the three traditional theological virtues—faith, hope, and love—help to shape a distinctive style of life in the world. Beyond this, however, the individual Christian must do his own improvising. The image of the "new humanity" prefigured for us in Christ is an open-ended

---

[12] *Church in a Marxist Society,* p. 73.
[13] Smith, *Secular Christianity,* p. 204.

image. It is an image which points directions but lays down no laws. This means that Christian existence is essentially a life of becoming, of creative innovation, of never-ending adventure—above all, of openness to the future. It is like "the dance of the pilgrim," free and unconstricted enough to respond spontaneously and freshly to ever new situations. Just as we saw that the work of Christ was, in a sense, provisional, so also the existence of the Christian always strains forward to new possibilities as yet unimagined, unrehearsed, and unrealized.

Faith: The Freedom to Risk Life

The fundamental structure of Christian existence is no more illuminatingly described than in Jesus' familiar paradox: "Whoever would save his life shall lose it; and whoever loses his life for my sake and the gospel's will save it" (Mark 8:35). An avant-garde psychologist, Norman O. Brown, has translated this truth into rather brash contemporary idiom: "The solution to the problem of identity is, get lost." [14] Rilke once said it another way: "That which would remain what it is, renounces its existence." What these statements add up to is simply this: Life must be risked, if it is to be won. The mature Christian is the man who has found the freedom to risk life, and who paradoxically receives it back again in more abundant measure than when he let it go. Bread cast upon the waters has a way of returning again to reward the giver.

This principle of risk is simply the working out in the Christian life of the "logic" of the cross and resurrection. It is a principle, moreover, which applies to all human life. That life comes only through death, that human fulfillment is a possibility only when life is abandoned reck-

[14] *Love's Body* (New York: Random House, 1966), p. 88.

lessly to values and goals which transcend the immediate self—this is a truth which men recognize in the depths of their being, even when they violate it.

One of the most poignant illustrations of this fact in contemporary literature is the story of the successful French lawyer, Jean Baptiste, in Albert Camus' *The Fall.* Walking home one night from a rendezvous with a mistress, he heard a splash in the river and shortly thereafter the desperate cries of a drowning woman calling for help. His soul froze within him, but he hurried on through the fog, fearful of the risks of getting involved. Saving his life, however, was not such an easy matter. For the rest of his days that dying woman's cry reverberated hauntingly in his consciousness. Years later, a wreck of his former self, he talked to his alter-ego over a beer in an Amsterdam bar: "Please tell me what happened to you one night on the quays of the Seine and how you managed never to risk your life. You yourself utter the words that for years have never ceased echoing through my nights . . . : 'O young woman, throw yourself into the water again so that I may a second time have the chance of saving both of us." [15] In that incomparable vignette, Camus has captured the experience of many others who "have managed never to risk" their lives, and whose humanity has been tragically diminished in the process.

What is the reason for this obsession of man to avoid the risking of his life? The theological tradition from Kierkegaard to Niebuhr has traced the problem to its rootage in the anxiety which man experiences as a creature who is both finite and free, as a being who stands at "the juncture of nature and spirit." While anxiety is the source of man's creativity, it is also, Niebuhr claims, "the inter-

[15] (New York: Alfred A. Knopf, 1958), pp. 69-70.

159

nal precondition of sin." [16] In Niebuhr's arresting simile, "it is the condition of the sailor, climbing the mast . . . , with the abyss of the waves beneath him and the 'crow's nest' above him. He is anxious about both the end toward which he strives and the abyss of nothingness into which he may fall." [17] This corroding anxiety tempts him either to exaggerate the possibilities of his freedom or to try to suppress it altogether. If he goes the first route, he becomes guilty of a promethean pride which seeks to bring all life under his control; this is the sin of the strong-willed man. If he chooses the second, he surrenders himself to slothful self-indulgence or immerses himself in undisciplined sensuality, while running from the perils and responsibilities of human freedom and self-determination; this is the sin of the weak man.

If this is an accurate representation of man's predicament, then the debate between those who would identify man's primal sin as *pride* (Niebuhr) and those who describe it in terms of *sloth* (Cox)[18] is surely ill-conceived. For both of these sins are rooted in an even more fundamental aberration of man, namely, his *unbelief*. It is because of the absence of faith in the transcendent Power which gives him his life and defines his destiny, that man resorts to these illicit and ultimately futile stratagems for dealing with the anxiety occasioned by his own ambivalence.

It is true that the historical situation in a given period may prompt us to see one or other of these basic expressions of human sinfulness as particularly dangerous. Cox may indeed be right when he identifies apathy as the car-

[16] Reinhold Niebuhr, *The Nature and Destiny of Man* I (New York: Charles Scribner's Sons, 1941), 182.

[17] *Ibid.,* p. 185.

[18] Harvey Cox, *On Not Leaving It to the Snake* (New York: The Macmillan Co., 1964), pp. vii-xviii.

dinal sin of our generation—a particularly deadly sin because it strengthens the grip of a repressive and conformist society by weakening the sense of individual responsibility for the shaping of human destiny. But a dehumanized society is the creation not only of those who accept their limits too readily and become apathetic cop-outs from the struggle for a better world. It is also compounded by those who seek to exceed their proper limits, and in their pride of power attempt to create a world on their own terms at the expense of others who must suffer from their rapacity and tyranny.

Both forms of sin are in fact opposite ways of coping with the gnawing anxiety which man feels in the face of life's ambiguities and insecurities. The one is expressive of an apathetic ego, the other of an expansionist ego. Each of them elaborates its own distinctive life style: the one symbolized by the sloth, hanging inertly from the branches of a tree; the other by Prometheus stealing the fire from the gods. But both of them are desperate attempts to find a basis of self-contrived security by renouncing the risk of life on God's terms.

Christian existence offers the possibility of breaking this compulsive drive for security and liberating a man for a life of genuine spontaneity and risk. If our diagnosis has been correct, such a liberation can come only from "a freeing sense of security" [19] which is a gift of grace issuing from beyond man himself. As Ebeling has written, "it is the mystery of human personal being that it is summoned from elsewhere, that it exists in response and as response, and that man is therefore wholly himself when he is not caught up in himself, but has the real ground of his life outside himself." [20] A man can know "a freeing sense of

[19] David C. Duncombe, *The Shape of the Christian Life* (Nashville: Abingdon Press, 1969), p. 22.
[20] *The Nature of Faith*, p. 115.

security" only when he experiences the transcendent ground of his being as Grace. Here is the secret of his salvation and healing—the knowledge that the ultimate reality with which he has to do meets him as Love. When God in Christ embraces us as the Gracious Neighbor, we no longer need to go on building our pathetic defenses or hiding behind our artificial masks in order to secure our threatened egos from collapse. The word that comes to us, as Tillich has said, is: "Simply accept the fact that you are accepted!" [21] In accepting the divine acceptance of us, we are able to find the "freeing security" of self-acceptance. Because of God's affirmation of us, we are free to affirm life and risk it at the same time.

The freedom to risk life is the foundational attribute of the Christian life style on which everything else depends. It is this freedom which Luther knew as the ability to "let goods and kindred go, this mortal life also." This is the freedom that Christians find modeled for them in the life of total abandonment and risk which characterized the ancient pioneer, Abraham. Turning his back on everything that was safe and tested and familiar, spurning the securities of home and the conventions of long-established habit, "he went out, not knowing where he was to go" (Heb. 11:8). Such is the freedom of true faith.

There is in the freedom of Christian faith more of the quality of Dionysian abandon than uptight church people have customarily been prepared to admit. The ecstatic life style of Zorba the Greek has much in common with Christian freedom. When Zorba criticizes the life style of his Apollonian boss, he might just as well be indicting many nominal Christians who have not yet won their way through to "the liberty with which Christ has made us free":

[21] *The Shaking of the Foundations*, p. 162.

162

"No, you're not free," he said, "The string you're tied to is perhaps longer than other people's. That's all. You're on a longer piece of string, boss; you come and go, and think you're free, but you never cut the string in two. It's difficult, boss, very difficult. You need a touch of folly to do that; folly, d'you see? You have to risk everything! But you've got such a strong head, it'll always get the better of you. A man's head is like a grocer; it keeps accounts: I've paid so much and earned so much and that means a profit of this much or a loss of that much! The head's a careful little shopkeeper; it never risks all it has, always keeps something in reserve. It never breaks the string." [22]

Zorba incarnates a way of being human which Jesus had occasion to praise in the most lavish terms. When Mary crashed a dinner party being given in his honor at the home of Simon the Leper in Bethany, she too surrendered to "a touch of folly" which broke the string of conventional propriety and inhibition. Holding over Jesus an alabaster jar of expensive perfume, she shattered it and allowed its precious contents to flow over his head. The "shopkeeper" instincts of the gathered disciples were scandalized by this act of extravagant abandon. But Jesus silenced their criticism with words of commendation: "She has done a beautiful thing to me. . . . Wherever this gospel is preached in the whole world, what this woman has done will be told in memory of her." (Matt. 26:10, 13)

[22] Nikos Kazantzakis, *Zorba the Greek* (New York: Simon & Schuster, 1965), p. 300. For a description of the difference between the Apollonian and Dionysian life styles, see Sam Keen, "Manifesto for a Dionysian Theology" in H. W. Richardson and D. R. Cutler, eds., *Transcendence* (Boston: Beacon Press, 1969). "The essence of the Dionysian way is that it dares the extreme and hence leads to a form of consciousness which is alien to the law-abiding and mean-regarding character of the Apollonian mind. The Dionysian way exalts ecstasy over order, the id over the ego, being possessed over a possessive orientation, the creative chaos of freedom over the security of inherited patterns of social and psychological orientation, and divine madness over repressed sanity." (p. 36)

No depiction of a Christian life-style for today can afford to overlook those words of approval of a Dionysian element of self-abandon in Christian existence. Christians are people who have been "freed up" sufficiently to "let themselves go" in expressing their true feelings. They are emancipated enough from inner fears and anxieties to make themselves vulnerable, to risk everything, in pursuing the master passion of their lives which they have caught from the contagion of Jesus Christ.

Hope: The Expansion of Life's Horizons

Ours is a generation hungry for hope. The apoclayptic events of our time have thrown us on the mercy of hope in a way unparalleled in our previous history. We are in real peril of becoming psychologically and spiritually immobilized by our fears of immanent disaster on an increasing number of fronts. "No world has ever faced a possibility of destruction," writes the famed physicist, Robert Oppenheimer, "comparable to that which we face, nor a process of decision-making even remotely like that which is involved in this." [23] It is not surprising that in such a situation of extreme danger to the human race, a failure of nerve and a freezing of morale should be the result. Ernz Benz graphically describes how the situation has demoralized the intellectual leadership of our day:

The generation of thinkers who came to the fore after World War II suffered the fate of Lot's wife. She looked back upon Sodom and Gomorrah. She could not look away from the picture of decline and destruction. She became mesmerized by the abyss of human aberrations, by sexual, social, and spiritual abnormalities which led to the destruction of Sodom.

[23] *The Flying Trapeze: Three Crises for Physicists* (London: Oxford University Press, 1964), p. 63.

. . . She got lost in the constricting numbness of fear and defeat and—she was converted into stone.[24]

The same ossification of spiritual consciousness must be the fate of all of us who are unable to lay hold upon resources of hope which are capable of expanding the horizons of life beyond what is immediately visible. It is a strong temptation for Christians, as for others, to liquidate their investments in the future and live from day to day on current drafts from a rapidly dwindling checking account. Moltmann has indicted existentialist theologians for this kind of foreclosure of the future which results in "the obedient servant of God" being transformed into "the figure of the honest failure." [25] The existentialist saint is a man who has no real hope for the future, but who tries to live with patient integrity and love with those who are his companions in suffering. He opts for a life style which, in terms of the images of the previous chapter, concentrates exclusively on the paradigm of Jesus as "the gracious neighbor," while ignoring the clues to be gained from his other roles as "joyous revolutionary" and "invincible pioneer."

Even as admirable a Christian thinker as Ronald Gregor Smith, whom I have had the occasion to quote approvingly a number of times, allows his existentialist predilections to attenuate the place and meaning of hope in the Christian life. "Faith," he writes, "is at no point able to anticipate the future. This is the tragic melancholy inherent in the reality of faith, that it has no fixed future which it may draw into its present forms. Faith does have a form peculiar to itself; but it is the form of hope, of expectation, of patient waiting upon the future which is given to it again

---

[24] *Evolution and Christian Hope* (Anchor Books; Garden City, N. Y.: Doubleday & Co., 1968), p. 226.
[25] *Theology of Hope*, p. 24.

and again by God. This is the style of faith, and it forbids us to demand or to expect any permanent and identifiable expression." [26] It is difficult for me to believe that a life-style marked by "tragic melancholy," and bereft of any concrete expectations for the future, can be identified as authentically Christian. In this vision of the Christian life, hope appears to be collapsed into faith and reduced to a "patient waiting" for whatever destiny God may choose to mete out to us, with little of the vibrancy of Christian expectation left.

The New Testament seems to project quite a different picture of the relation of faith and hope. "Faith is the assurance of things hoped for, the conviction of things not seen." (Heb. 11:1) In other words, hope pushes back the horizons so that faith has breathing space and living space. Hope gives breadth and scope to faith by pointing it to a life-giving future. Its fruit is not a "tragic melancholy," nor is its characteristic stance one of passive and patient waiting. Its eager anticipation of the future incites us to an active transformation of the present in the light of things which as yet are "not seen." This means that the stance of the Christian is typically both futuristic and activistic. Both elements are implicit in Paul's description of his own life style: "One thing I do, forgetting what lies behind and straining forward to what lies ahead, I press on toward the goal for the prize of the upward call of God in Christ Jesus" (Phil. 3:13-14). There is no authentic Christian life without that forward-looking orientation which mobilizes all our powers in the task of making "all things new." "Hope mobilizes. It puts together a disciplined surge toward the crack in the door of the future. And the remarkable thing is that time and again the door yields to a determined push." [27]

[26] *Secular Christianity*, p. 196.
[27] Fackre, *The Rainbow Sign*, p. 12.

Hope is able to expand the horizons of our life by empowering us to transcend the realities of our present experience. We are able to overcome the despair and tyranny of the present by, as it were, putting one foot into the future. This makes us, in a real sense, pilgrims and strangers on the earth, misfits in society, since we carry within our breasts a vision of hope which puts a subversive question mark over every status quo.

Some of the hope theologians have been inclined to conceive of this dialectic between present and future too much in terms of absolute contradiction. Thus Moltmann says: "Present and future, experience and hope, stand in contradiction to each other in Christian eschatology, with the result that man is not brought into harmony and agreement with the given situation, but is drawn into the conflict between hope and experience." [28] In this connection, he likes to quote Paul when he says that "hope that is seen is not hope. For who hopes for what he sees." (Rom. 8:24) There is danger, however, in relating present experience and future hope in terms of stark contradiction. There *is* real tension between present and future, but it is not the tension of absolute conflict; otherwise hope would be reduced to pure, groundless fantasy. Here one of Tillich's last lectures has a word of sound wisdom for us: "If a daydreamer expects to become something that has no relation to his present state . . . he is a fool. . . . Where there is genuine hope, that for which we hope has already some presence." [29]

It is the tension between present realization (which is always partial and incomplete) and future hope (which constantly outstrips the fulfilments of the present) that provides the motor and spring of Christian action and mis-

[28] *Theology of Hope*, p. 18.
[29] "The Right to Hope" in *The University of Chicago Magazine* (November, 1965), p. 17.

sion. This tension introduces an element of perpetual restlessness into the heart of Christian existence. As hope opens up ever new horizons of possibility, it invests every present with a profound unrest and discontent with things as they are. Moltmann describes well this divinely induced impatience of hope:

Faith, wherever it develops into hope, causes not rest but unrest, not patience but impatience, It does not calm the unquiet heart, but is itself this unquiet heart in man. Those who hope in Christ can no longer put up with reality as it is, but begin to suffer under it, to contradict it. Peace with God means conflict with the world, for the goad of the promised future stabs inexorably into the flesh of every unfulfilled present.[30]

The horizon-expanding power of hope is the Christian's answer to the apathy and inertia of our immobilized generation. It is the cure for the premature hardening of spiritual arteries and the deadly ossification of institutions. It makes possible a way of being human which is the enemy alike of personal mediocrity, social injustice, and institutional rigidification. Christian existence, as hope-filled "viatoric" existence, can be the means by which a society is jolted out of its lethargic and suicidal fixations in unjust and dehumanizing structures, toward genuinely creative human achievements of growth and transformation.

Love: The Affirmation of the Other

The crowning virtue of the Christian life is *love*. "So faith, hope, love abide, these three; but the greatest of these is love." (I Cor. 13:13) Above all others, love is the attribute which identifies unmistakably the true follower of Christ. "By this all men will know that you are my dis-

[30] *Theology of Hope,* p. 21.

ciples," Jesus said, "if you have love for one another" (John 13:35). Or, as the words of the popular folk-hymn express it, "They will know we are Christians by our love."

Whenever the authenticity of love has dominated the life-style of Christians, it has lent a credibility to their witness for which even the cynics have had no effective rebuttal. Citizens of the ancient world, we are told, were astonished by the quality of loving demonstrated by the early disciples. They could only exclaim: "See how these Christians love one another!" On the other hand, where love is lacking, the credibility of the Christian's profession of faith is decisively undermined. "If any one says, 'I love God,' and hates his brother, he is a liar; for he who does not love his brother whom he has seen, cannot love God whom he has not seen." (I John 4:20) That is why Christians who can indulge in racial slurs, or mouth chauvinistic war slogans, or stand in self-righteous judgment against the poor, are such a contradiction in terms as to be beyond belief.

We live in a world in which it is dreadfully easy to be cynical about love. Is a life-style characterized by anything remotely resembling genuine love a realistic possibility in a world so dominated as ours is by competitiveness and prejudice, conflict and hatred? Those who have had their humanity suffocated by discrimination and oppression are particularly inclined to be skeptical. James Baldwin gives us an inkling of the loveless environment which black people must endure in our country:

Yes, it does indeed mean something—something unspeakable— to be born in a white country, an Anglo-Teutonic, anti-sexual country, black. You very soon, without knowing it, give up all hope of communion. Black people, mainly, look down or look up but do not look at each other, not at you, and white people,

169

mainly, look away. . . . The universe which is not merely the stars and the moon and the planets, flowers, grass, and trees, but *other people*, has evolved no terms for your existence, has made no room for you, and if love will not swing wide the gates no other power will.[31]

Jean-Paul Sartre has developed a psychology of interpersonal relationships which makes love between human beings a literal impossibility. In his jaundiced view of human nature, men cannot relate to one another except in terms of perpetual warfare. Because the freedom of the other is always a threat to me, I must manipulate our relationship in such a way as to turn him into an object, and he in turn must do the same to me. Thus human intercourse is a continual oscillation between sadism and masochism, in which we violate other persons or are violated by them. As Sartre sees it, no one can really say "thou" to another in an experience of communion in which the freedom of both parties are affirmed. One of the characters in his play *No Exit* sums up succinctly the resultant human dilemma: "Hell is—other people" [32]

Sartre's analysis has the merit of enabling us to see with unusual clarity the consequences of a life-style from which love has been effectively eliminated. It poses some inescapable questions. Is a life-style in which men are constantly transfixing one another with objectifying gazes which turn people into things really a way of being human, or a way of betraying our essential humanity? Is our humanity truly represented when it is seen as a continuous cycle of predatory manipulations of other people in order to neutralize their threat to our claim to unlimited freedom? From the standpoint of Christian faith, this repre-

[31] *The Fire Next Time* (New York: Dial Press, 1963), p. 44.
[32] *No Exit and Three Other Plays* (Vintage Books; New York: Alfred A. Knopf, 1960), p. 47.

sents the very antithesis of what it means to be human. It violates man's fundamental nature as a creature made for love, destined to find his fulfilment in free, uncoerced communion with others.

God, who in his inmost nature is love, has placed the imprint of his image on the structure of man's existence. This is why men know, at least in their moments of greatest clarity and honesty, that they are created in love and for love and that love is the very law of their being. This is also why, after two thousand years, they continue to resonate to the image of Christ as the gracious neighbor. For they see in that image of a man abandoned utterly to the life of love their most credible clue to the mystery of ultimate reality and the meaning of their own existence.

What is love in the Christian sense? It is not a vague sentiment about which the romantics like to rhapsodize. Neither is it a rarefied, transcendent ideal, so exalted above ordinary human existence that it has no real roots in our human passions and longings. Much damage has been done to the Christian understanding of love by such misguided attempts to sentimentalize or idealize it. "The humanists suspect, and rightly," says Daniel Day Williams, "that the Christian view of love has become repressive, negates the full valuation of sexuality, sentimentalizes charity and neglects justice." [33] When this is allowed to happen, love loses it leverage on the concrete stuff of human relationships and becomes, at best, a pious irrelevancy, and at worst, a dehumanizing repression of our full human reality.

Here the old docetic heresy raises its head once again in a new guise. In his monumental study of Christian love, Anders Nygren has described the *agape* love of the New Testament in such a way as to make it a possibility for

[33] *The Spirit and the Forms of Love*, p. 13.

God, but not for men. The love which the Christian has for his neighbor is really not a human love at all, but the free, spontaneous, unmotivated love of God "infused" or poured into him and then poured out again upon his neighbor. It only *appears* to be the Christian man who does the loving; actually "the real agent is no longer the ego, but God, or Christ, or God's Agape, or Christ's Spirit." [34]

This cannot be viewed as anything else than a unfortunate dehumanizing of love. When Christian love is in this way removed entirely from the context of human motivations and affections, when the divine *agape* is set in opposition to the human *eros,* it becomes a superhuman, even antihuman, prodigy. No expression of Christian love is finally believable unless it wells up out of the springs of human emotion and passion as an authentic act of the self in reaching out and affirming other selves. As David E. Roberts once observed, "There is a direct connection between suitable 'erotic' expression and a man's capacity for Christian 'charity.' " "It is no accident," he added, "when ascetic saints find it impossible to put warmth into the neighbor-love of which the Gospel speaks." [35]

While Christian love cannot simply bypass human *eros,* neither can it be exhausted in it alone. The *eros* of human love all too readily becomes possessive, acquisitive, self-centered, concerned only for the pursuit of personal pleasure. It needs the purifying, transforming power of *agape* to redeem it from egocentricism and hedonism. When *eros* is transfigured by *agape,* it no longer manifests itself as the desire for conquest, the passion to draw everything into oneself. It assumes an other-regarding style of expression which affirms the "other" in his freedom, integrity, and uniqueness. Its goal is no longer a union of

[34] *Agape and Eros* (Philadelphia: Westminster Press, 1933), p. 98.
[35] *Psychotherapy and a Christian View of Man,* p. 136.

possessive absorption, but a communion of freely inter-acting selves.

To really love another person is to "let him be," that is, to affirm him in his unique possibilities of personal self-expression. The mature parent does this when he gives the child "breathing space" for independent growth, rather than smothering him with possessive affection. Bonhoeffer talked about this quality of Christian love in terms of "bearing the burden" of the one who is loved—not in the sense of taking over the responsibility for his life, but in affirming his freedom to be what he is in his weaknesses as well as his strengths. "To bear the burden of the other person means involvement with the created reality of the other, to accept it and affirm it, and, in bearing with it, to break through to the point where we take joy in it." [36]

When love is thus seen as a bearing with, and an affirma-tion of, other persons in spite of their idiosyncracies and inadequacies, it should be obvious that it cannot be sep-arated from suffering. Love demonstrates its fidelity when it is able to accept the pain of disappointment which denies its perfect consummation in the present. "If we look only at love's consummation we do not see it whole. Love has another mode, of faithful, courageous waiting for a con-summation, not yet realized. Love lives not from the ecstasy of fulfilment, but from a loyalty not yet fulfilled. Love realizes itself, not only in the enjoyment of comple-tion but in the suffering of the Not-yet." [37]

"The suffering of the Not-yet" leaves no room for the sentimentality of premature anticipation of the *eschaton* of love. That is why the life-style of the Christian includes the bearing of a cross. Love wins its victories only through conflict and suffering. The ecstasy of communion is not

[36] *Life Together* (London: SCM Press, 1954), p. 91.
[37] Williams, *The Spirit and the Forms of Love*, p. 14.

possible, whether between two persons or within social groups, without the risk of estrangement. Christian love is no cheap and tawdry sentiment which can be had at bargain prices. It demands the investment of our very life's blood in the quest for reconciliation and communion. This is what it took for Christ to be the gracious neighbor. And it is unlikely that we can get off any cheaper. "When Christ calls a man, He bids him come and die." [38]

If love is to reach these heights, it must find its sustaining roots in the other two theological virtues—faith and hope. It can accept the disappointments and continuing conflicts of the present because it has hopes for something better in the future. It can go on bearing with the realities of estrangement and alienation, buoyed up by the promise of the coming "beloved community" in which the perversions and distortions of our feeble human loves will be finally healed. It can exercise such audacious hopes for its consummation, however, only because it is sustained by a faith that our history is borne by a Love which transcends all human loves. In the final analysis, we have the freedom to love only when we are grasped and affirmed by a love which is greater than our own. "We love, because he first loved us." (I John 4:18)

Joy: The Celebration of Life

Joy is the inevitable concomitant of a life-style characterized by faith, hope, and love. These three attributes of the Christian life are not superfluous additions to our humanness which can be dispensed with without any real loss to the quality of our human life. They constitute, in fact, the *sine qua non* of the realization of our true humanity. They

[38] Bonhoeffer, *The Cost of Discipleship* (New York: The Macmillan Co., 1958), p. 73.

174

identify a way of being human which not only points to man's ultimate end, but participates in it here and now. This participation in man's true being, in however fragmentary a way, infuses life with an irrepressible joy. The festive celebration of life is thus the natural outcome of the style of being human which is practiced by the Christian.

This celebrative dimension of Christian existence has all too often been sadly lacking in the church. This may be symptomatic of the failure of Christians to experience in any conspicuous measure the fullness of human life promised in the gospel. Or it may reflect a distorted understanding of the nature of the Christian life which makes suffering and self-denial into ends-in-themselves that afford a special proof of saintliness. Kierkegaard, for example, was one who tended to see suffering as the definitive mark of faithful Christian existence. Whatever its cause, the Puritanical grimness of much Christian piety has made it a singularly unattractive option for those who are anxious to affirm the fullness of their humanity.

Let it be said with emphasis that the knight of faith is not "the knight of the doleful countenance" (Don Quixote)! He is more typically "the joyous revolutionary." He is, to be sure, no stranger to suffering. But suffering is always the minor key in a life style which seeks to appropriate Christ's promise of "abundant life" for all God's creatures. Let us be done then with those dismal caricatures of Christians as sad-faced, inhibited, shrivelled old ladies dressed in black! Christ came that we might "have life, and have it abundantly" (John 10:10). Christian existence must somehow reflect that life-affirming, life-celebrating goal if it is to give proof of its authenticity.

Christian celebration must, as I intimated in an earlier chapter, "toast all the daughters of time" (Cox). It remembers with festive joy those liberating events of the past that have provided the healing meanings and horizon-expanding hopes which enable us to be more fully human in the present and orient ourselves to the future with confidence. The celebrative life also provides us with a sensitive radar for the detection and enjoyment of the creative possibilities of the present. In this vein, Ross Snyder writes movingly of the humanizing significance of celebration:

Celebration is appreciating the possibilities hidden in the folds of life, even while being aware of all the evil and frustration that is there. It is believing that creation has good in it, and this good we invoke. Celebration is delight in the elemental simplicities— the deed well done, the thought well spoken, the beauty freshly seen, the relation of intimacy, the imagination inventing new dreams, the conversation striking fire, the body exhilarated.[39]

Celebration, however, must not allow itself to become so captivated by the satisfactions and joys of the present that it forgets the disparity which still exists between the "first fruits" and the final harvest of our redemption. Carl Braaten warns us rightly of the danger of "imagining full satisfaction in the present, relaxing the tension toward the futurity of the promise through the immediacy of false joy and dancing around a stationary god—a golden calf." [40] It does us no harm to remember that the Israelites' pilgrimage to the Promised Land ground to a halt when they were overcome by the ecstasies of Baal worship, when they allowed the intoxication of present satisfaction to dull their vision of a future still to be won.

This Baal syndrome is the peculiar temptation of the currently popular human potential and encounter group movements with their emphasis on sensitivity, body contact, festivity, and play. There is no denying the enormous benefits derived from many of these efforts to humanize people by putting them in touch with their honest feelings

[39] *On Being Human* (Nashville: Abingdon Press, 1967), p. 33.
[40] *The Future of God*, p. 48.

and tapping hitherto unrealized possibilities for a more rewarding personhood. The danger is that these nuclear communities can easily degenerate into secular pietism, becoming introverted and complacent in relation to the larger society. Celebrating the fulfillment of their own humanness in the intimate context of the encounter group, they can become quite oblivious of the aching unfulfillment of the world around them and the blatant dehumanization of masses of people less fortunate than they. It is perhaps no accident that this movement has had its greatest appeal among the relatively affluent segments of our society who have much more to celebrate than others whose humanity has been stunted by poverty and discrimination.

It is always a strong temptation to try to eternalize our experiences of celebration, just as Peter tried to settle down on the Mount of Transfiguration while evil spirits still held men in bondage in the valley below. It is only when our joy contains within it something of the eschatological tension which reaches forward towards even "better promises" for the future, that it is immune to the idolatry of premature satisfaction with the "utopia of the present." An eschatological joy is able to celebrate God's present gifts, while still experiencing something of the pain of the "not-yet." "I would expect from Christians, who believe in God's presence in the midst of revolution," writes Moltmann, "that they would laugh and sing and dance as the first to be liberated in creation." But this is a provisional celebration and not a final one. Christians will be "strange birds in the revolution," Moltmann goes on to say, because "they are deeply committed to it but also laugh about it." "They are deeply committed to it and laugh at it *because* they are the forerunners of a yet greater revolution, in which God will abolish even greater oppositions than any human revolution can envisage." [41]

[41] *Religion, Revolution, and the Future,* p. 146.

VII

THE CHURCH: VANGUARD OF A NEW WORLD

The struggle for Christian credibility in our time has, ironically enough, no greater enemy than the church itself. The fact is that most people's attitudes and responses to the Christian faith are shaped by their encounter with some particular expression of the church. If in its characteristic pronouncements and its basic life style the church projects a confused, innocuous, and unconvincing image, it can hardly be expected that it will generate much credence for its message. The history of much modern skepticism and atheism can be read as the story of honest and sensitive men reacting to caricatures of the Christian faith which they saw exemplified in the churches of their acquaintance.

While we have found other reasons for the crisis of contemporary belief, it is impossible to separate it finally from a growing crisis of confidence in the viability of the institution of the church. At a recent international symposium in Rome on "The Culture of Unbelief," Harvey Cox ventured the following pertinent observation: "It may be that the major reason for unbelief . . . is not that people find the gospel incredible, but that they find the Church incredible." [1] He went on to cite a variety of ways in which the credibility of the church has been eroded by the glaring inconsistency between its profession and its practice: a church claiming to serve the Prince of Peace, yet unable to act decisively against war, a church proclaiming the ideal of poverty, but continuing to amass great wealth

[1] *Unity Trends,* May 15, 1969, p. 10.

and real estate. The major religious problem of our time, Cox concluded, is not unbelief but hypocrisy.

It would be easy to add to Cox's catalogue of ecclesiastical hypocrisies. Who will believe a church which glories in the cross, the symbol of suffering servanthood, while fleeing from the filth and turmoil of the inner city to the peaceful haven of antiseptic suburbs? Or a church which insists on the oneness of all men in Christ, but nurtures some of the most virulent pockets of racism in our society? Or a church which sings and preaches about Christian freedom and joy, whose gatherings reflect an uptight, grimly moralistic conformism, devoid of human warmth and creative spontaneity? Or a church which acclaims the newness of life in Christ, while projecting the image of a tired conservatism, and clinging desperately to the symbols and habits of the "good old days"?

It would be futile and dishonest to gloss over the church's massive betrayal in our day of its true nature and mission. At the same time, it is important to recognize that this is not the first time that a "performance gap" has occurred in the history of the church. The discrepancy between what the church is supposed to stand for and its actual performance has always been sufficient to tempt men to cynicism. Robert McAfee Brown has drawn our attention to a late medieval manuscript in which appears these words: "The Church is something like Noah's Ark; if it weren't for the storm outside, we could not stand the smell inside." [2] That is hardly more flattering than indictments of the church of much more recent vintage which have made their debut under such disturbing titles as *The Comfortable Pew, The Noise of Solemn Assemblies, The Stained-Glass Jungle, The Suburban Captivity of the Church,* and *The Grave of God.*

[2] *The Significance of the Church* (Philadelphia: Westminster Press, 1956), p. 17.

The Paradox of the Church

The fact that the church is vulnerable to criticism as a human institution, sharing in the imperfections and ambiguities of all historical phenomena, should not in itself be sufficient to undermine its credibility. It is a misguided utopianism which gives up on the church simply because it exhibits no immunity from the distortions and frailties of other social institutions. We can protect ourselves against premature cynicism about the church only by a candid acknowledgment of its complete historicity and humanity. The church is frequently referred to in the New Testament as the people of God. This entails, among other things, the fact that it is a real human community, susceptible to the entire gamut of human foibles, conflicts, and sins. It is, moreover, a sociological community, characterized by the same dynamics and resistances which are encountered in other sociological groups. Insofar as the church is a human and historical reality, we can expect to find the same forces operative in its life as elsewhere to produce pettiness and power struggles, defensiveness and exclusiveness, dehumanizing routine and stifling organization.

If this were all that could be said about the church, however, we would have ample reason to ask about its credibility. It is always appropriate to address to the church the question "What do you more than these?" What unique and indispensable functions does the church serve in our common life which are not served by other social institutions? What distinguishing marks identify the church as something more than a custodian of the values of an old order that is passing away, and brand it as the pioneer of God's new age? What indications are there that the church listens to a different drummer than the "god of this world" which calls it to conformity to the standards and expectations of the prevailing culture?

In answer to these questions we must insist that the church is not only a *sociological* community which reflects in its humanness something of the distortions and imperfections of estranged human existence. It is also a theological community which continues to incarnate, however fragmentarily and inadequately, God's redemptive and humanizing purposes for all men.[3] "Once you were no people but now you are God's people." (I Pet. 2:10) Here is the foundational conviction by which the church is constituted: that God is calling out from among men a new community, a new people, which will serve as the spearhead of the new creation by which history is destined to be renewed and transformed.

We do not grasp the essence of the church till we see it as a paradox of divine action and human response. The church is, at one and the same time, part and parcel of God's redemptive action in the world and a genuinely human community responding faithfully though imperfectly to that action. Wherever a group of people struggle in the face of resistance to keep alive the vision of the new world and the new humanity which God is fashioning out of the old—there is the church. Wherever a community of faith responds to the action of God in Christ by exhibiting here and now tangible and perceptible signs of his coming kingdom of love and righteousness and peace, there you have a true body of Christ entitled to be called the church. A church authenticates itself as a true church by the measure in which the ferment of a divine discontent with things as they are keeps it from being domesticated as simply another functional unit of society.

[3] Cf. Tillich, *Systematic Theology* III, 165-72.

Escaping the Paradox: The Accommodationist Strategy

This paradox which defines the church's being generates, therefore, unavoidable tensions which at times threaten to become unbearable. In an effort to escape the trauma occasioned by these tensions, two characteristic strategies have been resorted to, both of which betray erroneous understandings of the church. I shall refer to these two attempts to escape the paradoxical reality of the church as the accommodationist and idealist strategies.

The accommodationist strategy is content to accept the model of a church which is simply one more social institution among others, accepting the roles assigned to it by its surrounding social milieu. Its existence is justified by its ability to cater to the psychological, moral, and religious needs of its members. Though it may pay deference to a certain amount of religious language and ritual, the church functions essentially as a social club where congenial friendships are forged, or as a center of indoctrination where the young are trained in the accepted social and cultural values of the community. Its primary reason for being is to provide a religious cement for a given culture and a religious sanctification for the social status quo. Taken to its extreme, this strategy leads to the loss of any real experience of transcendence in the church and the profaning of its life to the level of a purely sociological reality. The results of such a strategy are alarmingly visible in our time in the large sections of the church which have fallen into virtual cultural captivity, allowing themselves to become emptied of any distinctive theological substance which would keep them in tension with the norms and expectations of society.

The drift towards secularist accommodation has been accelerated, particularly in American Protestantism, by a popular theological error which effectively dissolves the paradox which is constitutive of the church's being. This is the voluntaristic understanding of the church as "a voluntary association of like-minded believers." In this view, the church is essentially a humanly contrived contractual arrangement for purposes of mutual edification and support of individuals who happen to adhere to certain common beliefs and objectives. Such a view, of course, has more in common with John Locke and his social contract theory of the state than with the New Testament understanding of the church. According to the latter, the church is not to be conceived as a voluntary organization set up to serve the essentially private moral and religious needs of a particular group of people. It is rather an essential part of the universal-historical activity of God aimed at creating a new humanity and a new world.

The tragic payoff of the voluntaristic error in ecclesiology comes in what Gibson Winter has called "the suburban captivity of the churches." Conceiving of itself as a voluntary association responsive solely to the interests and needs of its members, the typical Protestant church has joined the exodus of the white middle-class to the suburbs. Here it has formed a "homogeneous society of peers," re-enforcing rather than challenging the social insulation and stratification of the urban metropolis. It has become a haven of retreat from the bruising conflicts and harsh impersonality of urban living. People go to church in the suburbs for comfort, not for challenge.[4] Here the church fulfils the socially acceptable role of providing a sense of identity and belonging to an alienated social class, ministering to the private and familial needs of those who share common interests, cultural tastes, and ethnic characteristics. The

[4] Cf. Charles Y. Glock, Benjamin B. Ringer, and Earl R. Babbie, *To Comfort and to Challenge: A Dilemma of the Contemporary Church* (Berkeley: University of California Press, 1967).

result is the abandonment of any sense of responsibility to the wider urban community beyond the residential ghetto which makes up its membership, and with it, any valid claim to be the representative of God's reconciling mission in the world.[5] This ghettoization and privatization of Protestant Christianity, stemming at least in part from the mistaken notion of the church as a voluntary association of believers, has dealt a nearly fatal blow to the Christian credibility of the church.

Escaping the Paradox: The Idealist Strategy

The crisis in the church today is also compounded by those who, in reaction to the church's accommodation to the secular culture, are turning to the idealist strategy for escaping the tensions endemic to the church's existence as a sociological-theological community. They are the disillusioned idealists, many of whom make up the growing ranks of what the late Bishop Pike referred to as "church alumnae." Disenchanted with the institutional inertia of the church, its irrelevance and insensitivity to life-and-death issues of human welfare, its uncreative and conservative image, and its failure to assume a prophetic stance in society, they have opted out of the organized church. We dare not fail to see their protest as a profound judgment upon the widespread apostasy of the present-day church. Indeed, those who are most deeply loyal to the church will always keep this option open. The following

[5] Cf. Gibson Winter, *The Suburban Captivity of the Churches* (New York: The Macmillan Co., 1962), pp. 158-59: "Religious faith and practice have become a private sphere of American life—a sphere preoccupied with the emotional balance of the membership, the nurture of children, and the preservation of a harmonious residential milieu. . . . The inevitable consequence is social irresponsibility, which means that the churches have abandoned a context of public accountability in order to serve exclusively the emotional needs of selected groups."

184

statement attributed to a German theological student expresses a sound posture for Christians today: "We must
try to be at one and the same time *for* the Church and
against the Church. They alone can serve her faithfully
whose consciences are continually exercised as to whether
they ought not, for Christ's sake, to leave her." [6]

The urge to bypass the institutional church, however,
can be symptomatic of a false idealization of the church.
It can represent a romantic yearning for a "pure ideal" of
Christian existence uncontaminated by stultifying organization and limiting structure. It can be a new kind of
Puritanism which seeks the spirit without the body, or a
new form of pietism which is looking for a church which
is a company of the elite. Those who are tempted in this
direction, says James E. Dittes, "run the risk of becoming
the beatniks of the church, protesting against irrelevance
and disengagement by disengaging themselves still more
into isolated individualistic 'Greenwich Villages.' Perhaps
worse than the 'suburban captivity' of the churches is their
captivity in 'the village.' " [7]

That sort of value-judgment, it seems to me, reflects too
little appreciation for the contribution of the "idealizers"
and the "iconoclasts" whose gadfly role in summoning the
church to a more authentic Christian mission has kept
alive the ferment of an uneasy conscience and at least the
possibility of repentance and renewal. It does alert us,
however, to a strategical and theological error to which
the new breed of revolutionary churchmen are constantly
vulnerable. While the error of the voluntarist view of the
church lies in an oversecularization of the church which
leads to cultural captivity, the error of those who are ob-

---

[6] Quoted in A. R. Vidler, *20th Century Defenders of the Faith* (London: SCM Press, 1965), p. 122.

[7] *The Church in the Way* (New York: Charles Scribner's Sons, 1967),
p. 8.

sessed with the "ideal" church is to deny the real humanity of the church to the point of losing effective leverage on the ambiguous stuff of our common life. The assumption is often made, though less often explicitly articulated, that the "true" church is to be found somewhere else than in that imperfect, fallible, and sinning body of humanity which is bound to a lethargic institution and hemmed in by inhibiting structures. The true church, it is believed, has an unblemished mode of being which is somehow raised above the contingencies and ambiguities of history.[8]

Incarnation and the Ambiguity of the Church

In compromising the fully historical and human character of the church in the interests of preserving its transcendent purity, such views echo uncomfortably the old heresy of docetism. There is an ecclesiological as well as a christological docetism, and both of them manage to dissolve the paradox of the incarnation.

It is impossible to describe the church adequately except in incarnational terms. Paul's favorite metaphor for the church was the "body of Christ." Bonhoeffer defined the church as "nothing but a section of humanity in which Christ has really taken form." [9] Since the church has its being as the continuing embodiment in human form of the incarnate Christ, it is inescapably incarnational in its essential structure. This means that, just as God has chosen to act in and through the humanity of Jesus to pioneer and

---

[8] This tendency towards an ecclesiological dualism has found frequent expression in the history of theology, e.g. in the Calvinistic distinction between the visible and the invisible church, or the Barthian distinction between the "apparent" and the "real" church, or the distinction drawn by Brunner between the institutionalized church and the New Testament *Ecclesia.*

[9] *Ethics* (New York: The Macmillan Co., 1962), p. 21.

perfect a new humanity, so he chooses to call into being a people in whose humanly imperfect response his gracious humanizing work would continue to find expression in history. It is not, therefore, some transcendently perfect body, but the very human and blemished body which we call the church, that we must identify "warts and all" as the vanguard of the struggle to shape a new humanity out of the old.

It is basic to our understanding of the incarnation that we see in it the condescension of a God who makes himself dependent on vehicles of flesh and finitude to accomplish his humanizing purposes. The pulse of the divine life and love is able to reach us only by pushing through the phlegmatic, resistant tissues of our all-too-human corporate life. This means that incarnation necessarily entails risk. "That the church is called to be a human society means that the church is liable to the perversions of national, racial and class divisions. That God works through the church as human fellowship means that it can become merely an agency for warmth of companionship, for humanitarianism and for emotional release with a minimum of demands upon its membership." [10]

That God's saving word and action get incarnated in fleshly forms that are so riddled with ambiguity means that there is a certain inevitable "hiddenness" about the church. Just as there were those who failed to see the divine action and promise hidden in the creaturely existence of the man Jesus, so there are those who misunderstand the church through their inability to see the signs of God's working hidden in the historical particularities and institutional forms and human failings of the church as a sociological community.

[10] Claude Welch, *The Reality of the Church* (New York: Charles Scribner's Sons, 1958), p. 80.

This is the only sense in which it is theologically proper to talk about the church as invisible. It is invisible, not because it is some sort of transcendent spiritual entity which has a reality apart from the historical forms of community. It is invisible to the degree to which its true form never appears to us in outward and visible manifestation in an unambiguous way. Thus the outsider cannot be prevented from seeing it as simply a social or religious organization among other organizations subject to varying degrees of admiration or contempt, an ordinary group of people rather than God's chosen people, an ordinary body rather than the body of Christ, a sociological community rather than a spiritual community. "At best the Church can protest and confess, quietly better than loudly, that it is more than it appears to be. And above all, by living in faith, it can confront the world with the disturbing question: is there more here than appears on the surface?"[11]

Eschatology and a Church of Hope

The problem of the church's credibility is not, however, solved by affirming its paradoxical nature as an expression of the incarnation and its hiddenness under the ambiguous stuff of human existence. It is not enough to say that the church is somehow present in the midst of its distortions, though it is invisible except to the eyes of faith. Unless we are prepared to acknowledge that it is merely a matter of what is in the eye of the beholder, we must try to specify something of the concrete shape and image of the church which faith discerns as a credible reality despite its deformation in a greater or lesser degree in the actual churches. "Granted that we must view with the eyes of faith, we need also to ask, what does faith see? We have to inquire

[11] Hans Küng, *The Church* (New York: Sheed & Ward, 1967), p. 37.

what it is which God has wrought in the incarnation, in the creation of a new humanity and a holy people. What are the 'hidden' realities we confess, and how do they relate to the quite earthly and unholy realities so plainly evident to all?" [12]

A too easy assertion of the paradoxicality and ambiguity of the church can lead to an immobilizing complacency with the church as it is. Unfortunately, even a needed emphasis on incarnation can lend itself to a deadening conservatism in the church. Too exclusive a reliance on the incarnational principle can lead to a false kind of presentism which is totally preoccupied with the here and now.[13] This constriction of our horizon of interest to the present can encourage a servile acquiescence in the conditions of the status quo. The result is a church without creative tension with its environment, a church without a vision of future possibility, in a word, a church without hope. The principle enemy of such a church is change. The crowning testimony to its incredibility is the creeping boredom which infects its life like a terminal illness.

Tragically, this is what most people are in search of when they turn to the church—a Shangri-la of changelessness in a world of constantly erupting change. Carl Braaten is right on target when he identifies the nostalgic image of the church to which many are today wedded:

Perhaps the majority of people in our society think of the church as one of the last bastions of the old world. The church looks like a medieval cathedral and smells like a museum. And that

[12] Welch, *The Reality of the Church,* p. 38.
[13] Cf. Cox, *Feast of Fools,* p. 41: ". . . a needed emphasis on *incarnation,* the presence of the spirit in the flesh can, if overdone, lead to a kind of presentism, a total absorption of interest in the here and now. This presentism can in turn slip over into a supine acceptance of the world as it is, and the consequent disappearance of fantasy, hope, revolt, or vision."

is why many people still bother with the church. It gives them a handle on the old world to which they long to return. . . . The church is seen as an island of refuge from the maelstrom of change in the modern world. Those who cannot stand the bad weather outside may enter the sheltering asylum of the church.[14]

This image of the church as an institution which cushions us against the shock of change is being vigorously challenged today by a quite different perception of the church as a revolutionary vanguard of humanizing change in society. It is the conflict between these two incongruous images which is producing what Jeffrey K. Hadden describes as "the gathering storm in the churches." [15] In this increasingly bitter struggle, brought to a head by the church's involvement in the racial crisis of the sixties, the very meaning and purpose of the church is at stake.

The struggle for a recognizably Christian image of the church is receiving a great deal of impetus from the current revival of eschatology among the theologians. It is becoming increasingly evident that a one-sided incarnational emphasis must be corrected by a recovery of the notion of the church as an eschatological community of hope. The church is in desperate need of an image of itself which is potent enough and compelling enough to enable it to shake off the shackles of a sterile status quo-ism and break out of the bonds of its cultural captivity. Such a liberating image, I submit, is to be found in the biblical picture of the church as the pilgrim people of God. In a time of revolutionary change, this dynamic image of a nomadic people constantly on the move into an open future can perhaps more helpfully illuminate the church's self-understanding

[14] *The Future of God*, pp. 116-17.
[15] See *The Gathering Storm in the Churches* (Garden City, N. Y.: Doubleday & Co., 1969).

than the more static images of the church as a "body" or a "temple."

As a pilgrim community of hope, the church takes its cue from the experience of Abraham. He was the one who moved out courageously into unmapped territory because "he looked forward to the city which has foundations, whose builder and maker is God" (Heb. 11:10). The Abrahamic motif calls for a church which refuses to define itself in terms of institutional stabilities and securities. It calls for a church which is girded and goaded by the eschatological hope for a new and more human world that God is making, a new and more compassionate city whose builder and maker is God.

The pilgrim church sees itself as the vanguard and pioneer of that new world city which God is fashioning according to his promise in Christ. Its central business is to stoke the fires of hope which keep history moving towards its intended destiny in the kingdom of God's freedom and love. Its task is to erect here and there provisional signs of a renewed and redeemed future, and raise here and there anticipatory tokens of the new humanity which has already appeared in Christ and which God wills ultimately for all mankind. Insofar as it is animated by a living hope for the coming of God's new world, it sees its mission as that of breaking open the future in concrete ways which provide here and now credible demonstrations of what that new world will be like.

The Church, the Kingdom, and the World

The church as the pilgrim people of God can never be content to think of itself as existing for its own sake. Its very being is defined by a double focus which puts the center of its concern completely outside itself. The church is

191

not an end in itself; it is the servant of the kingdom and of the world.

What is here suggested amounts to a Copernican revolution in traditional thinking about God's saving action and the church's relation to it. The center and goal of that action is not the church, but the kingdom as it finds expression in the reality of a renovated and redeemed world. In fact, one day when the reign of God becomes fully a reality, the church is destined to become obsolete. Like the state in the Marxist utopia, it is scheduled to "wither away." In John's vision of the holy city, it must be remembered, there is no temple; with the fulfillment of the kingdom, the church as a separate institutional entity will become superfluous.

The revolution in thinking required here is dramatized in a slogan which came out of the World Council of Churches' study on "The Missionary Structure of the Congregation." This study suggested that we replace the formula "God-Church-World" with "God-World-Church." The purpose of this inversion is to make clear that God is first and foremost at work in the world, and the church's task is to join him there in his work of humanization and liberation. Contrariwise, it is not the church's role to incorporate the world into itself as the condition of its salvation. It is its much more humble calling to be an instrument and servant of God's mission in the world by being a sign which points beyond itself to the world's future.

This understanding of the church's relation to the world calls for a posture which puts the church's center of gravity completely outside itself. It is a stance which prohibits all ecclesiastical navel-gazing! The study cited above describes it as follows:

The Church exists for the world. It is called to the service of mankind, of the world. This is not election to privilege but to serving engagement. The Church lives in order that the world may know its true being. It is *pars pro toto;* it is the first fruits of the new creation. But its center lies outside itself; it must live "ex-centredly." It has to seek out those situations in the world that call for loving responsibility and there it must announce and point to *shalom*.[16]

The church proves her legitimacy only when she begins to pour herself out in loving, self-abandoning service to the world and allow the world and its needs to shape her agenda and her priorities. This does not mean, of course, that she is called to anything like peaceful co-existence with the world. It does mean that she is called, as Christians in East Germany like to put it, to live in *pro-existence* for the world.

To exist for the world means many specific things. It means to be *for* welfare mothers demanding a decent standard of living for their malnourished children; to be *for* young blacks turned into human derelicts by an economic system which denies them the dignity of a job; to be *for* migrant laborers robbed of the right of collective bargaining; to be *for* Vietnamese peasants forced into perpetual flight from bombs and bullets; to be *for* the generations yet to be born who must reap the bitter legacy of our irresponsible environmental pollution and our insane policies of nuclear escalation.

By and large, the church has grievously defaulted in its worldly mission. It has been governed by a set of theological presuppositions about the world which have served to cut the nerve of that mission. Pretty largely we in the church have been content to surrender the world to the devil. We have tried to fence off a little preserve in a protected religious corner of our lives where we believe that

[16] *The Church for Others* (Geneva: World Council of Churches, 1967), p. 18.

God is exclusively at work. Furthermore, we have allowed churchy speech and pious manners to incapacitate us for any meaningful communication and solidarity with those outside the church. J. C. Hoekendijk talks about the nervous embarrassment with which we typically encounter the worldly and the secular:

> How miserably unworldly, how piously and puritanically we have often gone about our work. For every worldly gesture a pious excuse had to be found immediately, for every token of solidarity we had a religious purpose. We tiptoed through the world with a perennially uneasy conscience, and we behaved as if all redemptive happenings exclusively take place within the institution of the church, and as if everyone should emigrate from the world to the church in order to be saved.[17]

It is hardly surprising that a church so self-conscious and introverted should suffer a shrinking credibility in the world.

The Servant Church

It is obvious from all that has been said that the true form of the church is always the servant form. The pilgrim church is not only the church of hope; it is also the servant church. Its model is the Servant-Messiah, the Gracious Neighbor who "emptied himself, taking the form of a servant," and who "became obedient unto death, even death on a cross." (Phil. 2:7-8) The governing principle of its life is summed up in the Greek word *kenosis,* or self-emptying. When asked for an account of its stewardship, it is not likely to point to the usual indices of institutional success—things like social status, growing membership roles, financial prosperity and physical plants. It is

[17] *The Church Inside Out*, p. 61.

more apt, like its Lord, to point to the scars in its body which are the credentials of its suffering servanthood.

There is a church known to the writer in a midwestern city which would never be written up in a "Who's Who of Successful Churches," but which over the last ten years has discovered what it means to be the servant-pilgrim church. Ten years ago it was one of the most socially prestigious and prosperous churches in the community, a church of some 850 members, able to claim some of the most prominent citizens in town as its members. Then the neighborhood began to change drastically as the black ghetto began to spill over and surround it. The church was wracked with controversy as its members struggled with the implications of the new situation. Within a short time most of the neighboring white churches had made a hasty retreat to the suburbs. But here was a church which continued to agonize over the meaning of a servant ministry and finally resolved to stand its ground and serve the needs of a multi-racial community.

That brave decision was costly in the extreme. In ten years the membership has gradually eroded to 165. The property is constantly scarred by vandalism, and members and staff are the frequent victims of petty thievery. Perhaps most painful of all has been the continuing alienation between friends and family members who have taken conflicting positions in regard to the church's future and its style of ministry.

Many would read the story of this church as a story of death and failure. I would prefer to read it as the heroic saga of a church which in the process of dying has been reborn into its true life as the servant people of God. Today the church has an integrated staff and an integrated membership, a rare witness in that city to the power of the gospel to reconcile men of different races. Its doors are open daily in a ministry to educationally disadvantaged children and high school drop-outs. Its small membership contains a disproportionately high number of those in the community who are active in working for social change and social justice.

The foregoing case study can be duplicated, I am sure, in many other places. One can find here and there in many cities churches prepared to risk their life in the ministry of the gracious neighbor. The moral of their story is clear. The church must die in order to live. It must die to its self-esteem, its presumptions of righteous superiority, its obsessive concern for its own wealth and prestige and security—if it is to be resurrected as the authentic body of Christ prepared to lay its life on the line for those who suffer and are oppressed. If the church is truly to become the servant church, it must be prepared to assume a level of risk-taking in its ministry to the needy of the world which will put its very life in jeopardy. "The church," says Richard P. McBrien in a recent book, "is entering a time when she must not only lose members but she must have the courage and the faith to promote actively their disaffiliation." [18] It will take no less than that kind of refining and purifying process to restore the lost credibility of the church.

The Exodus Church

To take seriously the pilgrim image of the church is to have done with, once and for all, all notions of fixity, permanence, and changelessness in our thinking about the church. The pilgrim church is always the exodus church, constantly moving out of its former bondages and securities, forever breaking camp and moving on with Christ to

[18] *Do We Need the Church?* (New York: Harper & Row, 1969), p. 207.

new engagements with those forces which would resist the pressures of his coming kingdom. "Therefore let us go forth to him outside the camp, bearing abuse for him. For here we have no lasting city, but we seek the city which is to come." (Heb. 13:13-14)

The tragedy of the contemporary church is that it has such an enormous vested interest in hanging on to its position of prestige and privilege in our society that it is often powerless to exchange its Egyptian bondage for the creative freedom of a genuinely pilgrim existence. Even though the age of Christendom is long since gone, the church still feeds on the nostalgic memories of that golden age of its Constantinian past when the church provided for society the stability and permanence of a sacred order. It turns to the past, not for the legitimate purpose of grounding its visions and hopes for the future, but for the illicit purpose of satisfying its lust for the permanent and abiding. "The church more often than not," Cox writes, "uses the memories of the saints not to encourage us in creativity but to bludgeon us into conformity. . . . It has discouraged radical fantasy as a possible threat to its hard-won place in Caesar's society. It cannot take the risk of putting its ultimate loyalty in the 'world to come,' . . . because it has too deep a stake in the world of yesterday and today." [19]

The church is often immobilized for its pilgrim journey simply by the sheer weight of overinstitutionalization. Bishop Robinson has forcefully reminded us of the "crushing investment in maintenance" which inhibits the church's freedom to move courageously in new directions: "It has the characteristics of the dinosaur and the battleship. It is saddled with a plant and a programme beyond its means, so that it is absorbed in problems of supply and pre-occupied with survival. The inertia of the machine is such

[19] *Feast of Fools*, p. 95.

197

that the financial allocations, the legalities, the channels of organization, the attitudes of mind are all set in the direction of continuing and enhancing the *status quo*." [20]

It should be obvious that the church cannot function as an exodus community as long as it is burdened by this kind of establishment mentality. Genuine exodus is possible only when we are prepared to give up the security of an established "place" in society and risk a really open future. If this is true, perhaps we can see the final death of a Christendom in which the church has had a guaranteed place of authority and prestige not as a cause for alarm but as a sign of hope. Perhaps we can even view declining financial support and shrinking membership rolls as an opportunity for the church to break out of its captivity to the Pharaohs of our culture and begin to find again its role as the vanguard of that new world which is promised in the gospel. Its credibility increasingly depends on its ability to liquidate its investments in the old order which is passing away and stake its very existence on the new age which is coming in accordance with the Christian hope.

Jan Lochman has testified that the church in Czechoslovakia has found unprecedented opportunities for a credible witness in the new situation of disestablishment: "It may be that a church which has no longer any privileges, and therefore no longer needs to defend itself, need no longer stand in its own way or in that of others, for in the post-Constantinian society the Christian can hardly be an opportunist. . . . You have nothing to gain by being a Christian. Rather you may lose. Thus the shadow of hypocrisy grows less. And here is the chance for a new credibility." [21] The church's unofficial establishment in American society continues to pose the grave temptations of the old Constantinian era. As long as church membership remains a

[20] *The New Reformation?*, p. 26.
[21] *Church in a Marxist Society*, p. 102.

social asset and not a liability, the charge of hypocrisy is inevitable, and the church's claim to credibility is bound to be suspect in the eyes of many. When the church is favored and patronized by the social and political establishment to the degree to which it is in this country, it should not be surprised when people draw the cynical conclusion: "The church speaks of God—but it means its privileges and those of its society." [22] Only a voluntary disestablishment through the conscious choice of the way of the cross, with all that that entails by way of a revolutionary challenge to the reigning presuppositions of the social and political order, can bolster its sagging credibility.

The Church of the Future

The reader will have grasped correctly the author's intent if by now he has drawn the conclusion that, in my view, much of the church as we know it today is doomed to senility and the creeping paralysis of inevitable death. No doubt many of the large and prosperous churches will continue to go through the motions of sycophantic service to the powerful and privileged elements of our society for an indefinite period of time. They will continue to eke out a captive existence at the pleasure of the social and political establishment, as long as they provide an aura of religious sanctity for its policies of repression and its pacification of social discontent. Such a role, however, cannot claim Jesus' promise concerning the church, that the gates of hell cannot prevail against it. And the church which chooses to sell its soul to the powers-that-be can expect to be at the mercy of the fickle whims of its opportunist patrons. For it, no enduring future is guaranteed.

Does this mean that the church has no assurance of a

[22] *Ibid.*

199

viable future? Not at all! Jesus' promise still holds good. Where there is Christian faithfulness, there is always the possibility that the Spirit can breathe new life into the dead bones of a moribund church. Repentance unto life is a possibility for churches as well as individuals. As if by miracle, the church has again and again been renewed in history through the agency of a "saving remnant." This dedicated minority has been unwilling to cry "peace" when there is no peace. It has forced the church again and again to break its unholy alliances with the dehumanizing forces of the status quo. Sometimes at the cost of martyrdom, always at the price of tension and conflict with temporizing ecclesiastical establishments, it has brought to birth new possibilities of faithful Christian existence within the church.

If the church is to have a future, we must avoid dealing with its current sickness with monolithic attitudes and strategies. On the one hand, we should resist the temptation to write the whole business off as beyond redemption, while investing all our energies in a brand new creation. There are still pockets of residual health here and there in the church which are capable of responding to a radical Christian ministry. Many churches are sleeping giants which can be aroused from their dormancy by the prodding of a prophetic and compassionate leadership. On the other hand, we should not waste our efforts vainly trying to resuscitate a dead body. Some churches should be allowed to die a natural death and given a decent burial. For there are no miracle drugs available which can do more than simply prolong their senile and unproductive existence. Their only reason for continued being is to swell the statistics on the chart of some church bureaucracy.

The critical situation of the church today calls for a plurality of options for those who mean business about their Christian vocation. There will be those who feel compelled in good conscience to move out of the existing church structures and participate in the development of new forms of Christian mission which are quite independent of the established churches. Such endeavors may well include many sensitive, turned-on people who have had no prior association with the church, but who are dedicated to working for a more compassionate and more human world. Most cities across the nation already have one or more of these experimental, "underground" churches. Rather than looking at this exodus with jealous disapproval, the established church might well be monitoring these new movements for creative suggestions for the renewal of its own life. They should be viewed not as esoteric showpieces, but as creative seed-plots for the development of new models of doing church in a radically Christian way.

It would be a pity, however, if all the creative and prophetic spirits were to emigrate from the church. This would not only confirm the church in its reactionary posture, but also abandon great potential resources for authentic Christian service and witness. If this potential is to be significantly tapped, it will require much more radical measures than heretofore contemplated. It will take dedicated cadres of revolutionary churchmen who function as highly disciplined pressure groups in order to force the church into a new integrity of Christian action and witness. These Christian revolutionaries must be sufficiently committed to persist in their demands for a costly reformation of the church, even to the point of divisive controversy and schism. For too long we have allowed the internal harmony and unity of the church to be our highest ecclesiastical priority, with devastating consequences to its life and mission. Today the stakes are too high to allow us the luxury of unity at the expense of the church's holiness. In any case, it is a spurious unity which immobilizes the church's prophetic ministry in the world. The risk of schism is the price the church must pay in recovering its credibility as a pilgrim-servant people.

It would be foolhardy to predict the shape of the church of tomorrow. Of this only can we be certain—that God continues to call out a people who will serve as the vanguard of his new world and the pioneer of his future. In whatever form God's faithful community emerges from the present struggle, it will have the continuing task of announcing and heralding the revolution that God is making in the world in order to assure the true destiny of men. It will provide in the authenticity of its own life and fellowship a demonstration model of the new humanity promised to all men. And finally, it will enter into the world as the servant-critic which seeks to prod and lure it on to its true consummation in the kingdom of God. The particular structures which implement these *kerygmatic, koinoniac,* and *diaconic* functions in the church of the future will undoubtedly differ greatly from what they have been in the past. That they continue in some form appropriate to the changing needs of the church and the world is a prerequisite of the church's survival.

INDEX

" I've chosen
a life-style of
out-rage — where
there is power & hope."
— an elderly woman
on life & celebrant
of sex until
rigor mortis